Stalking the Tiger
A Writer's Diary

by
Vartan Kupelian

Sleeping Bear Press

Copyright 1997 Sleeping Bear Press

All rights reserved. No part of this book may be reproduced in any manner without the express written consent of the publisher, except in the case of brief excerpts in critical reviews and articles. All inquiries should be addressed to:

Sleeping Bear Press   Sleeping Bear Ltd.
121 South Main   7 Medallion Place
P.O. Box 20   Maidenhead, Berkshire
Chelsea, MI 48118   England

Printed and bound in the United States

10 9 8 7 6 5 4 3 2 1

Cataloguing-in-Publication Data on file.

ISBN 1-886947-32-5

Contents

ॐ ॐ

Introduction

Cosmic Golf

*T*he Kid is Michelangelo and the golf courses of the world are his Sistine Chapel.

Eldrick "Tiger" Woods is an artist. His work is contemporary and the strokes are broad and bold. The artists of the late 19th Century popularized the notion of impressionism. On rare occasions, an artist comes along disguised as an athlete. Babe Ruth. Gordie Howe. Michael Jordan. Wayne Gretzky. Tiger Woods. At Augusta National, Tom Watson said, "Woods may be the type of player that only comes around in a millennium." But unlike the impressionist artists, these great athletes leave a mark not with small strokes to reflect light, but sweeping, kaleidoscopic strokes which embellish it.

In January 1997, Tiger Woods, age 21, already was an icon. His impact went well beyond golf and sports. It was universal. He traveled the world in 1997. The mission was to play golf, but his journeys weren't only about sports. They evolved into something quite a bit larger. That's Tiger Woods. Larger than life. The guy who plays cosmic golf.

That's also this book. Larger than what it was meant to be, what it was supposed to accomplish.

In January, at about the time Woods was embarking on his first full year on the PGA Tour, the purpose of this book was to chronicle his season for future reference. It was clear to me, as it was to so many others, that something out of the ordinary was about to take place. It was a simple deduction because, after all, there is nothing ordinary about Woods. As a golf writer, I knew it would be important to have a "Woods file," a compilation of notes, quotes, and anecdotes to which I could refer as needed during the year and for years to come.

The effort picked up steam through the early months of 1997. There was so much Woods material, so many angles to his performance and personality. Then came the stunning victory in The Masters at Augusta National Golf Club. Suddenly, there was no bigger story in sports than Tiger Woods, the phenom. He was on the cover of dozens of magazines, and most of them had nothing to do with sports. He was on television, in commercials, on billboards, in newspaper stories around the globe. He was getting invitations from President Clinton, buying a jet, making appearances at the All-Star Cafe, vacationing in Cancun, hugging royalty, and getting embroiled in controversy.

There were legions of supporters — and critics, too. The story had everything. The critics claimed there was a serious backlash building against Woods. The theory suggested that unless Woods was careful he would turn his adoring legions against him. I find that highly unlikely. It is a self-serving prophecy by those who, for whatever reasons, hope to see him fail, as a golfer and as a person. I've had several people tell me they were collecting anything that said that Woods would revolutionize the game — and that they would send it back to the authors and respective publications when he messed up.

My answer to that is simple. Tiger Woods could stop playing golf tomorrow and he'd already have changed the golfing landscape in meaningful and concrete ways.

Woods' impact has been enormous. Interest in golf? Up. TV ratings. Up. Attendance? Up. All this from a kid who looked into a television camera in August 1996, and said, "Hello, world." Hello, indeed.

More important than how many people are flocking to golf is who those people are. The demographics are new to golf. They are young, they are women, they are minorities, they are people who never liked golf before and maybe don't even like it now. But they like Tiger, and new customers are the lifeblood of any enterprise. It is an entirely new congregation. Fresh blood.

The staggering endorsement contracts he signed as a 20-year-old — totaling some $95 million — no longer seemed ludicrous as 1997 unfolded. On the contrary, Woods was beginning to look like a bargain.

There were so many things going on. Tiger Woods was everywhere and "the file" was growing.

This book is the file. It's a tournament by tournament look at Tiger Woods in 1997, a season during which he eclipsed the PGA Tour earnings record and became the first golfer to surpass $2 million on the regular tour.

But this book isn't just about golf, records, and money. I hope when you read it you'll agree it's about much more. Nor does it end with the final chapter. It's just the beginning for Tiger Woods. Michelangelo didn't create the Sistine Chapel in a year.

January

How the West Was Won

Mercedes Championship
La Costa Resort & Spa
Carlsbad, California
January 9–12

*I*t was the first Sunday of the 1997 PGA Tour season and the world was waiting for The Showdown. This was almost too good to be true. If it was like this in the first tournament, on the first weekend, what was the rest of the year going to be like? Fun, for sure. The downpours had transformed La Costa's pristine grounds into a rain forest and children of all ages were sloshing around in the puddles — some in expensive Dry-Joys, others in sneakers — like it was a school playground.

The world's best golfers waited in the locker room for a ruling. They watched television or chatted or read newspapers. The Mercedes Championship kicks off the PGA Tour campaign. It's an idyllic setting. Carlsbad is just north of San Diego, where the weather is nothing if it is not perfect.

Rain is seldom in the equation when tournament champions from the previous season gather for an invitation-only shoot-out. But now, with the rain continuing to fall, there was nothing to do and boredom had set in. Davis Love III needed to stretch. He lifted his lanky frame out of a chair and walked across the room. In his path stood Tiger Woods, and Love gave him a playful body block. It was akin to the initial contact — the first bit of action — that professional athletes need to brace for the upcoming battle.

And Woods, once again, was in the battle.

Woods won his first PGA Tour event in October 1996, at the Las Vegas Invitational, defeating Love in a playoff. That qualified Woods for the Mercedes Championship. Two weeks later, he won again at the Walt Disney World/Oldsmobile Classic. Woods almost needed a playoff in Orlando, too, except for the disqualification of Taylor Smith, who had used an illegal grip on his putter to match Woods' 72-hole winning score.

As the rain continued to fall in Carlsbad, it began to look like the Mercedes Championship was going to a playoff, too. Woods put himself in position for the playoff by finishing the third round in high style — four straight birdies in a 7-under-par 65. The final four holes at La Costa are called "golf's longest mile." Woods became the first player in the tournament's history to reach the 569-yard 17th hole in two shots, smashing a 260-yard 3-wood to reach the green.

Tom Lehman, the leader by 4 shots through 36 holes, had to birdie the final hole himself for a third straight round in the 60s. Lehman was the PGA Tour's Player of the Year in 1996. Lehman and Woods were tied at 14-under-par 202 through 54 holes and when the rain refused to stop, the inevitability of a playoff became reality just as Love and Woods were passing in the locker room. For Woods, it signaled the impending sudden-death fray.

The Showdown. The Player of the Year vs. the Rookie of the Year.

The best golfer in the world vs. the heir apparent, the prince who would be king. It wasn't the 18-hole shoot-out everybody had anticipated since the previous afternoon, but it would do quite nicely. Woods and his swing instructor, Butch Harmon, both in full rain gear, arrived on the driving range for the warm-up knowing the playoff hole would be the 7th — a par 3 measuring 186 yards. The hole was selected because it was one of the few playable holes on the course and didn't require a shot off a saturated fairway.

"Depending on the wind, it was going to be a 5- or 6-iron," Harmon said. "So for 15 or 20 minutes, we hit 5-irons, trying to hit just a slight draw. At first, he couldn't. He kept blocking them to the right. We made a minor swing adjustment by trying to let him sit a little lower with his arms on his through-swing so his arms could release a little better, and all of a sudden he hit about 30 of the prettiest draws you've ever seen, which was a perfect shot for the hole."

Lehman hit first. The ball shot toward the green, caught a breeze, made a sudden port tack and splashed. Harmon was amazed but he couldn't dwell on it. He quickly turned his attention over to his pupil — and the shot that won the west. "For people who were doubters and said Milwaukee and Las Vegas didn't have full fields or the best players in the world weren't there — well, they were all here this week," Harmon said. "And the results were the same."

Woods nearly holed his tee shot for an ace. He stuck a radar 6-iron nine inches from the cup and tapped in for a birdie and the victory, his third career PGA Tour victory in only nine starts. With it, the 21-year-old Woods reached $1 million in earnings faster than any player in history. The total: $1,006,594. Ernie Els, who previously held the mark, had needed 27 events to reach $1 million.

Typically, Woods expressed no surprise.

"No, this is what I set out to do — win every tournament. If my mindset was to make the cut, then it would be different. I'd be ecstatic. But I try to go out and win.

"The man upstairs was kind enough to give me a lot of ability."

Lehman put the victory, and the Woods phenomenon, in perspective. "I may be the player of the year for 1996," Lehman said. "But Tiger is the player of the next two decades."

Aces Wild

Phoenix Open
TPC of Scottsdale
Scottsdale, Arizona
January 23–26

*T*he PGA Tour starts each season with a western swing. It continues through the Tour Championship on the final weekend of October. But the golf doesn't end there. With the proliferation of silly season events — those made-for-TV productions featuring the biggest names in golf — precious little off-season is left for the marquee players. The Rocco Mediates, Jeff Slumans, and Fred Funks don't get invited to The Skins Games or The Shark Shoot-Out. Those are reserved for Fred Couples, John Daly, Payne Stewart, Tom Lehman, Greg Norman, and the other big names. So, with increasing regularity, the headliners who travel and play through December have extended their winter vacations into January and February. Still others, unimpressed with the importance of tournaments in Arizona and California, opt for lucrative appearance fees and glamorous outposts.

Couples played in the Australian Skins Game instead of the Buick Invitational in 1997. Two years ago, he won the Dubai Desert Classic and the Johnnie Walker Classic on the European Tour. Couples is not alone, of course, and the disappearance of such star figures has become a problem.

In recent years, the real start of the Tour has been considered the Doral-Ryder Open in Miami. It is there that they all gather, a month or so before The Masters, to begin the pilgrimage to Augusta National Golf Club and the first major.

The impact of a 21-year-old golfer on the West Coast swing was among the subplots in January. Already, by the admission of professional sports' most visible personality, Michael Jordan, and others, young Mr. Woods was becoming to golf what Jordan is to basketball — an icon. Jordan went so far as to call Woods his hero.

"As far as Mike saying that, I think Mike's great. He's an extraordinary person, not only for what he does on the court but also as a person, he's unbelievable. He's very nice and genuine."

Woods' absence from the Bob Hope Chrysler Classic, despite a personal invitation from Hope during a telephone conversation, touched off a ministorm. Woods was criticized for declining, especially since Hope had taken the time to call personally. Less was made of the fact that Woods declined an invitation from Nelson Mandela, president of South Africa, to play in that country's national open.

"It wasn't difficult because I had a prior commitment. He (Mandela) understands that. You always have to honor your commitments."

The controversy was short-lived.

As Tigermania swept golf, Woods tried to put it into perspective.

"It's interesting. I know who I am. My friends definitely don't treat me like this. I find it weird because I'm just like you guys. I'm a human being and all I do is chase a little white ball around."

Woods' second appearance of the year came at the Phoenix Open and, as usual, there was another subplot.

Phil Mickelson, the splendid left-hander, was Woods' predecessor as the world's next great golfer. He attended Arizona State, in Tucson, and the Phoenix Open was his turf. This was his home, and the battle between Mickelson — who swept Arizona in 1996, winning both the Tucson and Phoenix events — and Woods was hotly anticipated. It did not materialize.

The Phoenix Open, at the TPC of Scottsdale, belonged to U.S. Open champion Steve Jones, who blistered the field for an 11-shot victory. Jones' four-round total of 26-under-par 258 was one shy of the 72-

hole record set by Mike Souchak at the 1955 Texas Open. While Woods was never in contention, he still provided the most dramatic moment and a glimpse of Tiger Golf — the synergy between Woods and the gallery.

Woods — and a gallery's reaction to him — is electric. The current begins the moment he steps out of the clubhouse and continues until he leaves the premises. The buzz in the crowd is not unlike the constant buzz in high-tension wires, and the resulting force can be just as dynamic.

Fighting overflow crowds every step of the way around the TPC of Scottsdale during the third round, Woods finally arrived on the tee of the 155-yard 16th hole. The entire hole is an amphitheater, designed to maximize the effect of just such a moment. Estimates had up to 20,000 ringing the hole and, of course, the buzz reached a crescendo as Woods walked off the 15th green and toward the next tee.

The 16th hole already is recognized as one of the most festive spots on the PGA Tour, a fact quickly assimilated by young Mr. Woods, who recognized the aura — this was more like a college football crowd. He turned to his caddie, Mike Cowan, better known as "Fluff," and said,

"I should just run through the crowd like I was going through the tunnel into a football stadium...run up to the tee box and high-five everybody."

Well, he got his chance to do exactly that.

Woods drew a 9-iron out of his bag. The ball soared into the blue Arizona sky, pitched, and bounced twice...right into the cup.

The gallery went wild, and so did Woods. His celebratory posture included a couple of uppercuts, the pump, high-fives and raising the roof. The crowd littered the tee — which looked suspiciously like the end zone after an Arizona State touchdown — with papers and cans. The decibel count soared as high as the 9-iron shot that started it all, prompting a veteran golf writer to suggest that it may have been the loudest detonation in golf history. The crowd bowed and genuflected. It was uproarious. Andy North, two-time U.S. Open champion, was in the gallery. "It was the loudest roar I've ever heard at a sports event," North said. "The amazing thing is it went on for four or five minutes, from the moment he hit the ball to the time he walked up to the green and took it out of the cup."

"Right afterward, I don't really remember anything because I kind of went crazy myself. It was amazing. People were just going crazy. It's ridiculous how loud it was. I was oblivious to a lot at that moment. I was just trying to soak it all up."

It was the 10th career ace for Woods, and already his second on the PGA Tour. Later, in the lessening din, Woods was asked if drinks were on him.

"I'm broke."

Duel on The Beach

*T*iger Woods and Mark O'Meara are neighbors. One of Woods' first acts as a professional was to move to Orlando, which has become a popular home base for PGA Tour members. The weather is excellent, there's a world-class airport and nonstop routes to virtually every imaginable destination. And there's Disney World, where champions go to celebrate victories. Woods probably figured that if he lived in Orlando then every time he went to Disney World he'd be going home, too.

Once Woods settled into a home a couple of doors down the street from Mark and Alicia O'Meara, the veteran golfer became a close friend and, to some extent, a mentor to the youngster. They often practiced together and went fishing together. O'Meara is the consummate professional, and Woods gleaned every fragment of knowledge he could when they were together.

As a natural extension of their time together, they talked about someday going head-to-head. In other sports, it's called trash talking. In golf, it's a gentleman's challenge. It was during those practice rounds together that the wily veteran inevitably took some change off Woods — not that a couple of C-notes was going to send either to the nearest ATM machine. "He'll hole a shot [in a practice round] and get so fired up, pumping that fist," O'Meara said. "I've told him, 'Don't be giving me that fist deal. I'm going to bury you.'" The youngster's response was something like: Just wait until I get you when and where it really counts.

"He'd tell me that he can't wait," O'Meara said. "I'd say, 'Hey, Bud, I'm not going to back down. You might hit it 50 yards by me but I might find a way to clip you.'"

Woods' machismo was not misplaced. After all, he'd beaten Davis Love III in a playoff for his first PGA Tour victory, survived the stretch run of Payne Stewart for No. 2 and then stunned Tom Lehman in another sudden-death playoff at the Mercedes Championship for the hat trick. Woods was not only winning, he was knocking off the biggest names on the Tour. The question everybody was beginning to ask was: Is there anybody who can hold off this Tiger?

The answer was provided at storied Pebble Beach Golf Links and the narrator was, of all people, Mark O'Meara.

As with each Tour event, there were new experiences for Woods at Pebble Beach, where the pro-am format and celebrity status of the amateur participants puts an entirely different spin on the proceedings. Woods was assigned six marshals for crowd control and his courtesy car driver was handed a cellular phone to monitor his progress to the golf course.

Then there was the partnership — Tiger Woods and Kevin Costner. There had never before been a pairing quite like this. The biggest celebrity in the field, Costner, with the golfer whose celebrity status equaled the level of his game. The crowds were enormous and, frankly, they got to Woods. The tournament is played on three courses — Pebble Beach, Spyglass Hill, and Poppy Hills.

"I was down on Poppy and I could hear the crowd at Spyglass," Lehman said. "And that's like, what, five miles away? It was like, oh, Costner made another 3-foot putt."

The gallery didn't try to disguise its motives. "I want to see Tiger for the golf and Kevin 'cause he's a hunk," said a woman as a friend snapped a picture to validate her presence. "That's why I'm here."

Woods was to play in the National Pro-Am with his father, Earl, as an amateur partner. But the elder Woods had to cancel because he was scheduled to undergo heart bypass surgery.

How's this for an irony: The leading man, Costner, became the stand-in and made his intentions clear. "I didn't come here to finish second," he said. The sentiment matched Woods' long-standing approach.

"I try to win every tournament I enter. I see no reason to tee it up unless you have that attitude."

Woods was unnerved by the crowds, the attention, the noise, and the cameras. "It wasn't the professional photographers. You have to understand that," he said. "Pebble Beach is different than other events on Tour. We play with celebrities. Because of that, the Tour does not enforce the no-camera rule for spectators. You can hear the clicking during your backswing and downswing. They can get you at some pretty tough times."

He opened 70–72 and was in danger of missing the cut before sneaking through, tied for 67th. The third round, on Saturday, is known as "moving day" on Tour. The first test each week is to make the cut. Once accomplished, and another payday secured, the third round sets up perfectly for a big move. Some move up, others move down. Those who move up start thinking about a tournament title.

Woods' move was significant — he shot 9-under-par 63, one shot off the course record, and catapulted 62 spots. He went from 10 shots behind the leader, David Duval, to seven back; and from 67th to a tie for fifth. But it wasn't Duval he had to contend with in the fourth round.

It was his pal, O'Meara, and the finale was a classic, the drama withering even the most stouthearted. O'Meara, it should be noted, had an advantage. He'd won the National Pro-Am at Pebble Beach on four occasions, and his nickname, the Prince of Pebble, was not misplaced. O'Meara knows Pebble Beach like few others, and his affection for the glorious seaside course once described by literary giant Robert Louis Stevenson as "the most felicitous meeting of land and sea in Creation" is well-known.

O'Meara, three shots behind Duval, started the fourth round with birdies on four of the first seven holes to catch the leader.

Woods, playing directly in front of O'Meara and Duval, pulled to within one shot of O'Meara with a birdie from four feet at the 16th hole. At No. 17, the long par 3 to a kidney-shaped green, Woods turned to his caddie, Fluff Cowan:

"What do you think, Fluff?"

Cowan threw some grass clippings in the air, double-checked the yardage book and said, "Seven, stuff it."

"I said, 'Well, that's the decision. Let's go and stuff it.'"

Woods nailed the 7-iron to within four feet, and made that. O'Meara acknowledged the roar greeting Tiger's birdie with a chip-in birdie at the 16th, and said later, "That was a huge shot...the roar just motivated me more."

O'Meara reached 20-under-par, a tournament record, with another birdie at the 17th hole, while Woods was taming the normally unreachable 548-yard 18th hole with a driver–3 wood. The 18th at Pebble Beach is one of golf's great holes. It is bordered on the left by the Pacific Ocean. The tee shot must carry a portion of Carmel Bay that juts into the fairway. To get home in two requires a drive that cuts off a good bit of the dogleg and flirts with the Pacific Ocean. A more conventional play is safely down the right side of the fairway and three shots to reach the green. Hitting the ball right not only lengthens the hole but dramatically changes the angle of the approach shot and brings the Pacific Ocean into play. From that position, mere mortals don't see green. They see the shimmering waters of the world's greatest hazard. They see nothing but blue. It's an intimidating sight, enough to make almost everybody lay up when faced with the decision. But not Woods.

Using the lift, clean, and place rule that was in play all week because of the wet conditions, he put his enormous power on display. Fluff Cowan stepped off the distance.

"Front edge, 265 yards," Cowan said.

Woods nodded, the movement of his head barely perceptible, and drew a 3-wood out of the bag. He placed the ball — and smacked a 265-yard second shot to the front edge of the green. Cowan didn't flinch. He hoisted the bag on his shoulder and quickstepped to catch up to his man. Woods had an eagle putt but couldn't get it down. He made a two-putt birdie. O'Meara needed an up-and-down par on the 72nd hole to hold off the Tiger.

Woods offered credit where credit was due.

"I think it's great Mark won. I love him to death. But I'm disappointed. I should've been in a playoff if I didn't make that bogey (at the 13th). I made a run but it was too little, too late."

He paused for a moment and, in typical Generation X fashion, offered an assessment of the situation.

"Second sucks."

February

Asian Conquest

Asian Honda Classic
Bangkok, Thailand
Thai Country Club
February 6–9

*T*he journey to Bangkok, to borrow a phrase in '90s-speak, was *trippin'*. Translation: Out of control.

"After what I had to go through, I'm not surprised by anything anymore."

The whirlwind trip to his mother Kultida's homeland was bizarre in many respects and reflective of the Tiger phenomenon, the likes of which the tiny Omega Asian Tour had never before seen. The golf itself was almost an afterthought. Tiger won convincingly, by 10 shots, and there was never the possibility that he might not prevail. So that shifted the focus off the course and, for Woods, it was a kaleidoscope.

The blur of colors and activities began even before he got off the airplane at Bangkok's Don Muang Airport on February 5 following the 20-hour flight from Los Angeles. Even that seemingly simple routine of disembarking proved fraught with danger. Local Thai reporters, their cameramen in tow, stormed the airplane and actually boarded the jet searching for the first sound bite from Tiger. The week was sound bite heaven for the Thai media. Everywhere Tiger and Kultida went, reporters and cameras followed. Even street merchants were interviewed. "I like the Tiger Wood," said a Bangkok vendor. "His picture makes my sister scream."

The tournament director described a circus atmosphere, and observers called Tiger's visit the most celebrated event in Thailand since Michael Jackson's 1993 visit. Woods tried mightily to keep his composure. He did well in this regard.

Woods won first-prize money of $48,000 and received an appearance fee 10 times that amount in a tournament that had a total purse of $300,000. The appearance fee was downgraded as the week went on, as organizers appeared to be increasingly embarrassed by reports of the $480,000 figure. It didn't reflect well on them or Woods, and an attempt was made to "reduce" the appearance fee by providing the "correct" amount to selected media. In most quarters, the redress fell on deaf ears. After all, it made for an intriguing sidebar to the fairy tale just the way it was.

If Tiger was harried in Thailand, his mother Kultida was in all her glory. Tiger's motivation for the trip clearly was to please Tida, and she was pleased. If Tiger was the crown prince of Thailand for a week, Tida was the queen mother. Tida met Tiger's father, Earl Woods, who was a lieutenant colonel stationed in Bangkok, in 1971. She grew up 70 miles north of Bangkok, not far from the famous bridge on the River Kwai, which was the inspiration for the movie classic.

In America, Tida Woods always defers to Earl, but in Thailand the roles were reversed — and would have been even if Earl had been on the trip. Tida was easy to spot with her tiger-striped visor. She gave interviews and signed autographs, probably more than Tiger himself, and talked about her son's religious orientation. Tiger was raised in the tenets of Thailand's national religion, Buddhism, by Kultida. "He has an inner peace on and off the golf course," she said.

Kultida had been in Thailand for more than two weeks preparing for her famous son's visit. During an appearance on a popular TV talk show, she had referred to Tiger's status as an eligible bachelor and, of course, it made international headlines. Tida said she preferred a Thai bride for her son, "but this is a new generation and you can't choose for them... Whoever she is she'd better love golf because it takes up 99 percent of his time." The speculation floored Tiger and, gently, he confronted his mother. "All I said is that it would be nice if he did," Tida said.

"I will marry whomever I fall in love with."

Here are some other things Tiger had to contend with in Thailand:

- Lost luggage, which, according to a published report, "sent... Nike representatives into severe swoosh withdrawal."
- Stomach problems.
- A tropical heat wave which forced him to quit after 13 holes of the pro-am.
- Criticism for failing to make an appearance in the interview area after his 64, brought on by suggestions that for such a hefty appearance fee he should avail himself of such small inconveniences.

But the "upside" was worth the trouble.

Chavalit Yongchaiyudh, prime minister of Thailand, conferred honorary citizenship upon Woods on the floor of the Government House. His fame continued to spread across the globe and his understanding grew of what it means to be a celebrity.

"I've kind of gotten used to it. I had to go through it every week last year when I turned professional, and this year it has increased. I've been able to adjust."

He proved it with his golf over the 7,016-yard Thai Country Club layout. His rounds of 70, 64, 66, and 68 made a 20-under-par 268, and while most of his challengers were nondescript Asian PGA Tour pros, there were three notable exceptions. The best Steve Elkington, Curtis Strange, or Frank Nobilo could do was get within 13 shots of Woods.

The galleries weren't awe-inspiring by Tiger's American standards, but 5,000 golf watchers was monumental in Thailand, which has about 200 courses and one million golfers. Tiger's visit was expected to spur the development of more courses, with at least one estimate placed at some 60 more under construction or in early stages of planning. The media exposure was a godsend for the Asian Tour. There were 300 credential requests, or six times the 1996 attendance. The press room was standing room only.

"Winning, period, is great, but to win here in Thailand is something special. It was a hard week with a lot going on, a lot of different forces on me, so I'm proud I overcame that, too."

Crocodile Woods

Australian Masters
Huntingdale Golf Club
Melbourne, Australia
February 13–16

*D*one in, Down Under.

Peter Lonard's victory at the Australian Masters — where the winner gets a gold jacket, not green — capped a marvelous comeback from a debilitating injury. And while it took two sudden-death holes for Lonard to prevail over fellow Aussie Peter O'Malley, Lonard's measure was established during the third round at Huntingdale Golf Club. That's when the club pro from Oatlands in Sydney went head-to-head with the precocious American Tiger Woods and won the battle. Twenty-four hours later, Lonard would also win the war.

Woods opened with a 68. Despite holstering his driver and settling for a much more conservative game plan, he had the attention of the galleries. It didn't sit well with his playing partners, Brett Ogle and Robert Allenby, who would have liked to exile Woods to the Outback. At one point, Ogle snapped, "Tiger's not the only one playing out here," when the gallery began too quickly to move after Woods had hit.

Woods backed up the 68 with a 70 and was in position and poised to make a move. Lonard, a club pro paired with Woods, was to be the sacrificial lamb in the scenario. But Lonard fired a third straight 69, four shots better than Tiger, leaving Woods the sheepish of the pair.

Still, Woods wasn't out of it, and when none of the leaders put any distance between themselves and a slew of contenders, Tiger still had a chance.

"I could shoot a low round. If I can build momentum going into the back nine, who knows?"

But a Sunday charge never materialized, and Woods shot 73 to finish in a three-way tie for eighth with fellow American Larry Mize and Australian Rodger Davis, 7 shots behind Lonard.

The Australian press depicted Woods' performance as giving a good account of himself and "worth his appearance money" of $300,000, or more than double the first prize check of $125,000. It brought Tiger's take in appearance fees on the Asia/Australia trip to more than a half-million dollars, and perhaps much more, depending on which reports were accurate. But the cash was no use on the greens at Huntingdale.

"I couldn't buy a putt. The fact was that I misread a lot of putts and did not trust the lines. Then, all of a sudden, I didn't trust my stroke. Unfortunately, that's what happens. This week it happened to me. I wouldn't say there was a time when I have felt less confident with my putting.

"My stroke felt pretty good. I didn't have any complaints with that, but I felt unsure of my line. When you feel unsure about that, your speed is going to be off and you are not going through the putt with any authority."

Woods also noticed a technical flaw in his full swing.

"I know exactly what I'm doing. It's just that I can't stop it. It is something that I need to hit a lot of balls to get out of and I don't exactly want to hit a lot of balls in this heat. I noticed it [in Thailand]. It happens when you play a lot in the wind. It is very difficult because your swing is going to change when you play in heavy wind. Every time I go to Scotland, I come back with a different swing."

Lonard's career was interrupted in 1992 by Ross River fever, a malaria-like disease spread by mosquitoes. He left the pro tour Down

Under to work at a club job at Oatlands in Sydney while recovering, and became the first club pro to win the Australian Masters, which had been won six times in the previous decade by Greg Norman.

"The mosquito has been forgiven," Lonard said. "Those couple of years, I thought, 'Bloody hell, what's going on?' But I made a lot of friends. From the down times I have found who the real friends are. It probably has been good for me. I've seen life from both sides of the fence. I don't think I will ever get carried away with being a golfer because, basically, you are just chasing a white ball around. I've learned a lot from it."

Woods learned from the Down Under experience, too.

The putting woes validated the advice Woods had received from the other players regarding the nuances of Huntingdale's greens that local knowledge was an absolutely critical element to success.

"I learned a lot this week. Some of these putts look like they are going one way and go the other. Augusta is exactly the same."

Young Tiger Woods already had Georgia on his mind.

Family First

Nissan Open
Riviera Country Club
Pacific Palisades, California
February 27–March 2

*T*he next stop on the PGA Tour for Tiger Woods was scheduled to be the Nissan Open at famed Riviera Country Club in Pacific Palisades. But first he had to deal with his father's health. Earl Woods underwent heart bypass surgery on February 19. The operation was termed successful, but four days later, after a complication, additional surgery was required. Earl Woods first had quadruple bypass surgery a decade before. He was taken ill during the Tour Championship in October 1996, at Southern Hills Country Club in Tulsa, Oklahoma, and doctors determined that another bypass was necessary.

Tiger waited until the last minute to enter the Nissan Open, waiting to make sure his father's condition was improving. Once the tournament began, it was clear that Tiger was troubled.

"Golf isn't my main priority right now. It's kind of hard to play with my dad in the hospital."

His mood and play reflected the concern. Still regrouping after the Pacific sojourn, he wasn't sharp, but that's the magic of Woods. Even at something less than his best, he has so much game that he's always a threat. He opened with back-to-back 70s, for 2 under par, and kept himself in position to go low on the weekend. The charge never materialized. It stalled Saturday when Woods shot 72. A final round 69 left him tied for 20th at 3 under — a good week's work despite the distractions. Englishman Nick Faldo picked up his first win on American soil since the 1996 Masters.

It wasn't an easy week in another respect — there were more run-ins with photographers. This time, however, they were professional sports photographers, not fans clicking Instamatics and disposable cameras.

"It's ridiculous."

The whole scene led to the obvious decision that Tiger would not play the following week at the Doral-Ryder Open — the first Florida stop on the PGA Tour — which is regarded as the official kickoff to The Masters five weeks later. Tiger's revised schedule before Augusta now had Arnold Palmer's Bay Hill Invitational and The Players Championship the last two weeks of March, then a week off and then The Masters.

March

Long Live the King

Bay Hill Invitational
Bay Hill Club & Lodge
Orlando, Florida
March 20–23

*T*he Bay Hill Invitational is Arnold's tournament and, out of respect for the King, everybody shows up. Even the King himself.

It was the perfect setting for Palmer, who had undergone surgery for prostate cancer, to return to competitive golf. He was sidelined 42 days, during which the outpouring of respect and love only validated Palmer's place in golf lore. It was an interesting juxtaposition: Palmer, the King, returning to his own piece of golfdom, and Tiger Woods, the Man Who Would Be King, returning to the PGA Tour to join in the revelry and the occasion.

The fact is, there hasn't been a golfer since Arnold Palmer burst onto the professional golf scene with his first victory in the 1955 Canadian Open who has stirred the emotions and passions and revitalized golf like Tiger Woods. Jack Nicklaus is the greatest player of all time, but it wasn't until later in his career that the masses accepted Nicklaus. The reason is that Nicklaus was the man who challenged and threatened Palmer's reign. In some respects, the masses rejected the purge and withheld their consent until there was no longer any doubt or debate about Nicklaus' place in golf history.

There has been no such reluctance to embrace Woods, whose appeal transcends traditional golf boundaries. Woods' impact has been staggering because the stage is so much grander and because of the changing nature of society. Golf plays in a global theater today.

Therein lies a most discernible difference between Palmer, a public man, and Woods, a private man.

The point was underscored at Bay Hill when the April issue of *Gentlemen's Quarterly* hit the newsstands. Even before the article appeared, Woods and his representatives at International Management Group were decrying the methods used by the publication and condemning the story.

GQ portrayed Woods as a messiah, but not a messiah without flaws. In an unguarded moment, Woods begins to tell lewd, racially stereotypical jokes. The author also paints an unflattering picture of Earl Woods, and that more than anything else is what upsets Tiger. The consensus among the journalism fraternity that covers golf was that the article was overwritten and underreported.

"I have learned my lesson. I had to learn it the hard way. I have learned that some [writers] have an agenda going into an article — some more than others."

The firestorm was brief, although the issue would linger in a less volatile form, and it would become a subject for discussion between Palmer and Woods. Palmer has become an advisor and counselor to Woods, a guidance figure with no personal motives. Woods confides in the King, who offers his wisdom with no reservations. When Woods complains about the burden of fame and fortune, Arnold explains. For Palmer, the issue is not a reigning king or a young icon, the issue is the game he cherishes. It is still uplifting, still glorious, after all these years.

Palmer's message is unchanged through the years — to preserve the tradition, heritage, and integrity of the game. At times, he is concerned for the welfare of his sport. "I suppose it does scare me occasionally when I think that we are losing some of that," he said. "I hope we aren't. It pleases me to still be part of that. And I just hope that when Tiger Woods has been here for 42 years, that he can sit here and say the same thing to people coming on behind him."

The comparisons between Palmer and Woods are obvious. So is the generation gap. "You can't make a total comparison, simply because 42 years ago or more, it was a little different than it is today," said Palmer, whose first endorsement contract was worth $5,000 — piddling next to Woods' combined $50 million-plus haul from Nike and Titleist. "But in some ways, the process was the same then as it is now. As far as your private life is concerned, and your business of doing what you want to do, there have to be some sacrifices. There's not any way that you can be a person such as Tiger Woods or anyone else in that category that isn't going to have to pay some price for the monetary gains as well as the personal gains that you have.

"As you know, I visit with Tiger," Palmer continued. "I'm not going to tell you all the things we talked about, but one thing he said to me was that his public won't let him act like a 21-year-old man. Well, how many 21-year-old men are in the position Tiger Woods is in? I said, 'Hey, that's the price you must pay for the position you're in, whether it be financially or as a champion. There has to be a penalty somewhere for all the nice things that happen to you.' I never considered it a penalty, really. Most of the people in the world that I know are people I met through the game of golf and I consider them friends. So it's more than a penalty. It's a reward in addition to the financial and personal successes you have. I met my wife through golf and I've met most of my friends through golf."

For Woods, golf is the easy part of the equation.

"That part I love. Anything else, outside of the golf course, can be a little difficult at times. Whether it's people wanting a 10-second stop with you or an interview for ten minutes, or whatever. It's like people just want to get a piece of your time. Unfortunately, there are only 24 hours in the day and I can't please everybody. Sometimes you have to learn how to say no. That's one thing I've had to learn."

Woods wasn't a factor at Bay Hill. He shot bookend 68s, with a couple of 71s in between, to finish at 278, 10 under par. The title went to Phil Mickelson, who knows all about the pressure of expectations. Once upon a time, Mickelson was golf's fair-haired young superstar, and although he won four times in 1996 somehow he is still perceived as someone who hasn't achieved greatness. Mickelson's final-round charge at Bay Hill was reminiscent of Palmer's finishes in his heyday, of which Mickelson was reminded. "I'd seen a couple of pictures in the locker room with Arnold holding that putter up and giving it the Arnie charge," Mickelson said. "I thought it'd be kinda cool if I was able to do that...to emulate the master." Mickelson, three shots behind leader Omar Uresti midway through the final round, made his charge with a back-nine 30. "It's special because it's here at Bay Hill at Arnold Palmer's tournament the week that he came back," Mickelson said.

A Good Walk Secured

The Players Championship
TPC at Sawgrass, Stadium Course
Ponte Vedra Beach, Florida
March 27–30

By the time Tiger Woods arrived in Ponte Vedra Beach for The Players Championship, the PGA Tour was on full alert. Security measures outlined in a memo to tournament directors were being scrutinized and implemented. The PGA Tour was determined that Woods' tournament experiences would not be a good walk spoiled. He had plenty of company as he strolled the fairways at the TPC at Sawgrass Stadium Course. In fact, the entourage had a presidential flair. Woods got the superstar treatment.

"We have a huge marshal contingent, sheriff's officers, and even the Secret Service," said Brian Goin, the PGA Tour's general manager for championship management. "Large crowds are following him. All we're trying to do is help him through. The young man has business to do."

Woods' presence lured huge galleries to PGA Tour events. The Players Championship bumped its daily ticket allotment 5,000, to 35,000, and was sold out earlier than ever before. The increased security measures were designed to help move things toward normalcy and help Woods get around the golf course — right down to using kitchens and other secured areas as uncongested escape routes.

"At times it can get out of hand. Some of the past tournaments it's been tough just moving and you've got to draw the line some-

where because I'm obviously here to do a job. It's my job now and I try to be as accommodating as possible. But sometimes people don't understand. Therefore, we have to go to these measures and it helps me out a lot as far as getting around. I think it helps the other players, too, who are playing with me or playing behind me because it also speeds up play."

The state of alertness, Goin said, was close to the maximum measures ever undertaken by the PGA Tour. "We've had to handle this type of situation before with some of our marquee players when they were at the top of their games," he said. "We've gone as far as figuring out different ways of getting him to the range so as not to have people waiting each day. You've seen movies of [VIPs] walking through kitchens. It's not going to be the same [route] every day." Included in Woods' entourage was a retired Secret Service agent, Joe Corliss, and the golfer's own full-time security guard.

Englishman Nick Faldo, who knows a thing or two about being hounded by the media and other pitfalls of celebrity status, tried to sort out the Woods phenomenon at The Players Championship. "There is just something about him," Faldo said. "There have been a lot of players that have been famous for their aggressive, no-fear style. He has come on with a whirlwind...much more media attention. I think that has a lot to do with it, just the media hype of the whole thing. The impact Palmer and Nicklaus had coming on the Tour — great golfers, great men — and Tiger's no different, yet the media attention has made it into, you know, massive.

"He has made a major impact on pro golf," Faldo continued. "We all know the attention he's getting and what he is bringing. Some areas, it is good; some areas, it is bad. But generally it has given golf a boost. I know it comes at a good time. I know the commissioner (Tim Finchem) is working on TV rights this year and so he has got a trump card." It would be a huge trump card indeed.

Security wasn't the only problem the PGA Tour had to deal with regarding Woods' presence. Woods was getting so big that any tournament he didn't appear in was imperiled. It was one of the "bad" areas Faldo had mentioned. The non-Tiger Tour events were getting second-class treatment by the media. It was almost as though the tournament didn't exist. Even without Woods in the field, tournament stories featured him...as being absent. It didn't take a marketing genius to figure out there was a problem looming.

Steve Elkington didn't need a trump card at The Players Championship. He had an ace up his sleeve and cruised to a 7-shot victory over the best field in PGA Tour history to win The Players Championship for the second time. Elkington, the 1991 winner, posted four straight rounds in the 60s for a 16-under-par 272. Scott Hoch was next at 279. Elkington pocketed $630,000, plus a 10-year exemption on the PGA Tour.

"I basically blew away the best field we've ever had," Elkington said.

Woods, playing in the Tour players' championship for the first time, had an unremarkable tournament. He could do no better than 71 in any round and finished at 1 over par.

April

The Green Jacket

The Masters
Augusta National Golf Club
Augusta, Georgia
April 10–13

The allure of sports is not limited to America. The magic is universal. We are entranced by the golden moments of sports because they are so unpredictable that they challenge the basic truths of life and the alignment of the stars. Of course, that's what elevates them to heroic proportions, like Ulysses in Homer's *Odyssey.* Ordinary journeys are not recorded for posterity. Ordinary athletes and ordinary people are not the stuff of legends. O.B. Keeler didn't make a career covering mere mortals. He chronicled the life and times of Bobby Jones.

America is starstruck, and when golf's newest, biggest star, Tiger Woods, and his pal, Mark O'Meara, arrived at Augusta, Georgia on Monday of tournament week, nobody could have anticipated the epic proportions of what lay ahead at famed Augusta National Golf Club. The results challenged Homer's classic — the great record book was rewritten and the ensemble cast of characters rivaled major Hollywood productions in size and stature. Woods arrived as one of the pre-tournament favorites, along with Nick Faldo, Phil Mickelson and perhaps even Greg Norman, although The Shark's many springtime disasters in Georgia made plenty of observers leery. Not so with Woods, who would be making his first start at The Masters as a professional, and defending champion Faldo, a three-time winner.

Woods and O'Meara were among the last to disembark in Augusta, but that did not reflect on Tiger's level of preparation. It was diligent, precise, and complete, and his meager practice time at Augusta National wasn't the beginning — rather it was the culmination of those efforts. Woods' "homework" consisted of two phases — off-course and on-course.

He studied films of past Masters at The Golf Channel studios in his hometown of Orlando to make up for his inexperience at Augusta National. He paid particular attention to pin positions and greens and how some of the great champions of the past played the course, and other nuances. He took measures to assure that his putting would be finely tuned to Augusta National's slick greens — and he took some money off his pal O'Meara.

"I busted my tail to get ready. Mark knows about my putting in private and all the balls I hit, working on a few key thoughts. And when I came here, I was ready to go. I think Mark sensed that I was pretty confident in my playing abilities."

O'Meara had firsthand knowledge of the state of Woods' game. In a Masters warm-up match at Isleworth, their home course, Woods shot 59, including a mere 27 strokes through nine holes, and was 10 under par through 10 holes. From the tips, Isleworth measures 7,179 yards and is par 72.

"You know your game's ready. But that doesn't mean a whole lot when you come to Augusta, because you've still got to perform. And this golf course can take anybody who's confident and humble them quickly."

Woods called it an "easy" 59. He had irons into two par 5s (531 yards and 528 yards, respectively) and walked off each green with only a par, so it's not hard to imagine what the number might have been.

The expectations of Tiger were suffocating. Here was a 21-year-old being tossed into the mix of favorites, alongside Faldo, and some were going so far as to suggest Woods was the man to beat. There is no record of sportswriters ever being so smart, so insightful, ever before in history. Woods did not allow the expectations or the burden to affect him or his game.

"To be honest with you, I don't care what anybody else says. I just came here to win. Is it realistic? I think so. I don't know if anyone else does. If things go my way, I might have a chance to win this tournament."

Woods, who had studied Augusta National and The Masters like a history major cramming for an exam, knew that not since Fuzzy Zoeller in 1979, had a first-year participant at The Masters won the coveted green jacket. This would be Woods' first tournament appearance at Augusta National as a professional, and third overall. He played in The Masters in 1995 and 1996 as the reigning U.S. Amateur champion. He was ahead of the curve.

"Fuzzy won here on his first try. It can happen. Just depends."

Little did Tiger know that in a matter of days he would become embroiled in controversy with the man he used as an example.

৶ঽ

*F*or the opening round Thursday, Augusta National was set up to test the mettle of the world's finest golfers. But when the winds kicked up, it became a survival test more than a test of skills.

Tiger Woods made the turn at 4-over-par 40. He didn't notice the throng between the 9th green and the 10th tee. He was too busy lecturing himself for sloppy play.

"I was pretty hot at the way I was playing. I couldn't keep the ball on the fairway. From [the rough], you can't attack some of these pins. I was just playing real defensive golf, and that's not exactly what you want to do when you're struggling. It was a tough day initially, but I got through it."

Tiger, the survivor. He toured the back nine at Augusta National, and its Amen Corner, in 30 strokes, and the 2-under-par 70 left him among the first-round leaders.

"It was just a matter of driving the ball well. I knew what I was doing wrong, so it was getting out of that and trusting the motion from there. The tee shot on 10, I felt I was in a good position. I just tried to carry that swing feeling all the way through the back nine, and it worked. I was fortunate enough to have it happen on the 10th tee."

Woods was in contention, but the dominant story of Round I was the course condition — hard and fast, as usual — and the treacherous greens. It was fitting that the first-round leader was someone who didn't even have to pull his putter out of the bag on the 18th green. All John Huston did is hole out a 190-yard 5-iron shot from the wrong (10th) fairway to shoot 67, for a one-stroke lead over Paul Stankowski. Paul Azinger, looking for his first victory since the 1994 PGA Championship, was another shot behind at 69, followed by Woods.

"I'm just glad to get this round behind me. After the way I struggled on the front nine it was a good way to finish."

The greens were impossible. Ken Green had a five-putt on the 16th hole. Greg Norman missed a downhill six-foot putt at the 2nd — and had a 66-foot putt coming back. Nick Faldo — who had only one three-putt green out of 72 holes in 1996 to win the Green Jacket — had three-putts on four of the first six holes. Loren Roberts, a master putter who is known on the PGA Tour as the Boss of the Moss, had 40 putts. Tournament officials acknowledged that the high winds made the course, and the pin positions, much more difficult than had been anticipated. They admitted that, given the same circumstances again, they would probably have cut the holes in different spots.

Stankowski's preparation no doubt will be emulated in future years by others in the field. He cleaned the floor of his garage and practiced putting. "It's a 1½-car garage," Stankowski said. "I wish I had a 3-car garage so I could practice those 30-footers. It was just like putting these greens — hit the ball and walk behind it until it stops."

Woods didn't require such finesse. He simply overpowered Augusta National. There is no better example of how he muscled the course than the 500-yard 15th hole, a par 5 with a second shot over a pond. Tiger drove the ball 349 yards and was left with 151 yards. He used a wedge for his second shot, and made eagle. The normal range of clubs for the rest of the field was anywhere from a fairway wood to 4- or 5-iron. A few of the longer hitters got home with 6- or 7-irons.

"I just tried to draw a wedge in there and I did."

Woods started the first round with a bogey when he drove into the left trees, and then left his second shot in a greenside bunker. He also bogeyed the 4th, 7th, and 9th holes. The sequence resulted in the self-scolding behind the 9th green. It paid instant dividends — a birdie at the 10th, where Tiger hit a 2-iron off the tee on the 465-yard par 4, an 8-iron to 15 feet, and then drained the putt.

The rally picked up steam at the 13th hole, Amen Corner's signature par 5. The hole is easily reachable but the second shot must avoid the meandering Rae's Creek, which cuts diagonally from front left to back right. Woods ripped a drive off the tee and made a two-putt birdie. The four-foot eagle putt at No. 15 put him 4 under on the back.

Woods picked up on the survivor theme.

"I'm tight every tournament I play, because I care. The time you're not nervous is the time you quit, because that means you don't care anymore. Obviously, this is a big tournament. I'm going to have some butterflies, and I did. My swing wasn't quite there. Even on the range it wasn't there. I knew the swing key I needed to work on. It's really hard to trust it once the gun goes off."

The Woods-Faldo pairing didn't produce fireworks. Woods dominated, and the stoic Faldo, in an amazing twist, did not make the cut.

"We talked a lot more than you might think. I don't know if it's me or not, but he opens up to me and starts talking occasionally. You know, the exchanges we had were, granted, brief. But from what everyone tells me, it's different from the so-called norm with Nick."

Call it the Tiger Woods effect. There are new norms in golf, even at Augusta National.

For those needing more proof of Tiger's power, Woods supplied it in Round II with a surge that reduced the sacred ground to his own personal playground. He played the four par 5 holes in 5-under-par and shot 66–136, good for a 3-shot lead over Scotland's Colin Montgomerie, the European No. 1, and 4 shots better than Italy's Costantino Rocca. In a place where foreign domination has been a sore spot among Americans, it was shaping up as Tiger against the world.

And the world didn't have a chance. Montgomerie, who would play with Woods in the third round, knew the situation.

"It all depends on Mr. Woods," the big Scot said. "The way he is playing, this course tends to suit him better than anyone else. Still, there is more to it than hitting the ball a long way. The pressure is mounting. I have more experience in major golf than he has. Hopefully, I can prove that."

Woods averaged 336.5 yards off the tee in the second round. He hit a 4-iron into the 555-yard second hole, drove within 15 paces of the 360-yard third, and on the 455-yard 11th hole he used a sand wedge from 105 yards. He hit a 7-iron into the 485-yard 13th hole and made an eagle from 15 feet, and again drove 350 yards on No. 15, hitting a wedge from 150 yards to 12 feet for a two-putt birdie. In between he birdied No. 14 after hitting a 115-yard sand wedge to three feet. His total on the back nine through two rounds: 10 under par.

Woods, unlike just about everyone else at Augusta National, was unimpressed by his position through 36 holes.

"It's what I came here to do — try and win the tournament. I'm at the halfway point. I'm in the lead, which is nice. But as I said, it's only the halfway point. I need to go out there and shoot a good number tomorrow — because it's moving day — and get myself in a good position where I'm in good shape going into Sunday."

The difference between Woods' two previous appearances at The Masters — as an amateur — and his professional debut was remarkable. Tiger had an explanation.

"When I came here as an amateur, I was just coming off finals at Stanford. That's not easy. And because of that, I couldn't practice. I was pulling all-nighters trying to get ready for finals, and then I'd come to Augusta. That's a great way to try and get ready for The Masters. So, of course, I'm going to be at a disadvantage compared with the pros who have been playing week in and week out who are tournament-tough. This year, I have the same advantages they have. Now I feel just as comfortable as they do coming here.

"I'm pretty happy with the way I'm playing. Overall, I'm striking the ball well. I'm positioning my irons well so I can go ahead and take a run at some of these putts or just two-putt and move on. But I'm not forcing the issue like I did the last two years."

The third round belonged to Tiger Woods, but it was Colin Montgomerie who provided the most revealing and most insightful analysis of a most unlikely scenario. Montgomerie once had a reputation in Europe as someone who pouted. It earned him the tag of "Montglumerie" but he has since grown to be an articulate and personable fellow when he wants to be. Seldom has an athlete spoken fewer words and said so much as Montgomerie did late on that Saturday afternoon at Augusta National.

The third round ends about 6:30 P.M., and that means a tight early deadline for most of America's large Sunday newspapers. By 6 P.M., the serious fidgeting begins in the media room. Stories, with lead paragraphs that try to capture and summarize the occasion eloquently, are written and rewritten. Golf writers assigned to cover The Masters, in their finest display of mental gymnastics, try to break down the lead story, the sidebar stories, and the notebook items, knowing that time is running out and the copy desk at the newspaper back home is poised to rush the package of stories into print.

An early sidebar is a godsend for the beat writers. A quick later sidebar is like hitting the lottery. On that Saturday afternoon, Colin Montgomerie was a heavenly savior when he arrived in the interview room after his round with Woods. A day before, Montgomerie had talked about testing the youngster, putting on some pressure to challenge his mettle and see what he's made of.

The implication was clear. Montgomerie was the wily veteran, hardened by years of intense competition, and Woods would be on his turf now, in the heat. In fact, some weeks earlier, Montgomerie had said that he, for one, would love a piece of Woods at the Ryder Cup Matches and he knew of others on the European side who felt the same way.

But it was Montgomerie who was sweating after Round III of The Masters — figuratively that is. He shot 74, to Tiger's 65. It was Monty who had wilted when the heat was turned up, not Tiger. At the podium in the interview area, Montgomerie wasted little time with ceremony.

"When you add it all together, he's nine shots clear," Montgomerie said. "And I'm sure that will be higher tomorrow."

Monty was only warming up. He was about to write an entire sidebar for the print media.

"All I have to say today is one brief comment," he said. "There is no chance. We're all human beings here. There's no chance humanly possible that Tiger is going to lose this tournament. No way."

Flashback to 1996, the final round at Augusta National, where the swing between Nick Faldo, the champion, and Greg Norman was a whopping 11 shots. Woods' lead was only 9 shots. An emboldened reporter mulled those numbers over and asked, "What makes you say that?"

Montgomerie, the world's No. 3 ranked player, couldn't resist a smile and a crack.

"Have you just come in or have you been away? Have you been on holiday and just arrived?" he said. "This is very different. Nick Faldo's not lying second. And Greg Norman is not Tiger Woods."

Sidebar story complete. Thank you, Monty.

Greg Norman, the world's top-ranked player, is not Tiger Woods. Woods wasn't worrying about mathematical possibilities.

"The only thing I want is a green jacket in my closet. Whatever I have to do to win is fine."

Tiger shot 65, nobody made a run, and suddenly he had a nine-shot lead over Costantino Rocca of Italy, with Paul Stankowski another shot back and veterans Tom Kite and Tom Watson 11 behind.

"I told my pop someone was going to make a run, shooting at least a 66. I'm a little surprised no one made a run. But the tournament is not over yet."

Rocca, the nearest pursuer, was nearly as glib as Montgomerie. Asked if he had a chance, the Italian said, "Maybe if I play [only] nine holes — and under par, too."

"I've grown up a lot since the last time I played here. I've had to deal with a lot of things. You know, it's definitely toughened me up. I understand how to play a lot smarter. My course management is much better than it was even, say, six months ago when I turned pro. So it's come full circle. I'm hitting my irons, controlling my distances well, and I'm actually thinking well. That's a good combination.

"But the tournament's not over yet. Granted, that's a pretty big lead and I'm playing well. But, still, I need to go out there tomorrow and shoot a good number. I need to drive the ball well, think well, and play well. It's going to be a tough day tomorrow thinking about all the things that could happen. But I think that my experience — I'm going to draw upon Thailand as part of my big experience to handle tomorrow. Thailand, I had a huge lead going my last day, and I think I shot one of my best rounds in a long time, and won by 10. So that's something for me to think about tonight and look forward to going into it tomorrow."

The debriefing of Woods went on for quite some time. Once again, he was asked what a victory at Augusta National would mean to him.

"It means a lot, I guess for a number of reasons. It means a lot because I would have won. I would have become the youngest to ever win. But I think more importantly, in my estimation, it's going to open up a lot of doors, a lot of opportunities, and draw a lot of people into golf who never thought of playing the game. And I think on this kind of stage and this kind of media, I think it's going to do a lot for the game as far as minority golf is concerned."

Just as Colin Montgomerie had suggested, all that remained for Sunday's final round at Augusta National Golf Club was the coronation of Tiger Woods, the youthful master. Woods, 21, became the youngest winner at The Masters and the first minority golfer to win a professional major tournament. He didn't just win, either. He blitzed the field and dominated a daunting golf course like no one — not Hogan, not Nicklaus, not Palmer — ever has.

It was a Masterpiece.

"It is something I've always dreamt of — I always dreamt of playing in The Masters and winning it. It means a lot to myself, my family, and to anyone who knows how much I wanted to win this tournament."

As a nation sat entranced in front of the television, Woods shot a final round 69, for an 18-under-par 270 total, to win the 61st Masters by a record 12 shots over Tom Kite. Woods' rounds: 70-66-65-69. The TV viewing numbers were equally impressive. Ratings were up 53 percent over 1996, with 44 million people tuning in to see the triumphant final round. CBS ratings for The Masters were 14.1, with a 33 share — the equivalent of 13.7 million homes — compared to a 9.2 rating, 21 share, and 8.8 million homes the previous year.

Woods' total bettered the mark of 271 shared by Jack Nicklaus (1965) and Raymond Floyd (1976). The victory margin was the greatest in history — Nicklaus won by 9 shots in 1965. Woods narrowly missed equaling the greatest victory margin in a major championship in 135 years, since Old Tom Morris won the British Open in 1862 by 13 shots. Seve Ballesteros was previously the youngest champion at Augusta National — the Spaniard was 23 when he won the first of his two green jackets in 1980.

"Tiger is playing another game," Nicklaus said. "He's playing a golf course he'll own for a long time."

Woods' victory came two days before the 50th anniversary of Jackie Robinson breaking baseball's color barrier. Woods calls Robinson one of his heroes. Robinson made his Major League debut on April 15, 1947.

The green jacket so coveted by Woods was draped over his shoulders, in the tradition of The Masters, by defending champion Nick Faldo, who had to wait around for two days after missing the cut. He wandered around Augusta National virtually unnoticed by Tigermaniacs. "Phenomenal performance," said Faldo, the three-time champion and a man of few but well-chosen words.

"I think what we will see, with my age and influence I've had on the game, more young people will start to play the game. That barrier, young people not pursuing golf, now kids will think golf is cool and will start playing it."

The accolades flowed. Nicklaus, who won six green jackets in his storied career — more than anybody else, was most gracious. He had predicted that Tiger would win The Masters more than he, Nicklaus, and Palmer combined — 10. The golf record book, once written by Nicklaus, now was a blank page waiting for a new author. In his first assault on Augusta National, Woods shattered record after record, among them the lowest 72-hole score, 270, and the largest victory margin, 12 shots. Both records had been held by Nicklaus.

"My record? I'm not worried about that," Nicklaus said. "They're made to be broken. Tiger is dominating, is what he's doing. Take a look at the scoreboard, that'll tell you.

"He's a solid player. He knows how to win."

Kite, the runner-up, said, "Tiger has a wonderful golf swing and it's incredibly fast. What he has is similar to what Jack had in the '60s. He was way out in front of everybody else. Over the next 20 to 25, 30 years, everybody on Tour caught up to him. Well, this seems to be the next generation. Tiger has leapfrogged the rest of the field in terms of distance and he seems to have all the other stuff."

Kite waited by the 18th green as Woods marched home. "I wanted to see him finish," Kite said. "It's a very historic moment. That was an incredible moment."

Added Tommy Tolles, another of the contenders left in Woods' wake: "To hit it 300 yards, 320, 350 — however far he hits it and still keep the ball in play...what is there to say? We're not the main attraction now. Tiger is center stage and he definitely deserves it. This is a tournament he can probably win for the next 20 years. If he's on top of his game the rest of us are teeing it up for silver medals. We've got to improve on other aspects because Lord knows we can't hit it as far as he can."

Ben Crenshaw, a two-time Masters champion who cherishes the game and its traditions, called the triumph one of those special moments that separates Augusta National from all other places. "I think it is very appropriate that it comes here, at a magical place where these fabulous things happen," Crenshaw said. "I've always thought a lot of things happen here for a reason."

If he didn't already know that, Crenshaw discovered it two years earlier when he won his second green jacket. He had arrived at Augusta National with his game in disarray. The next day, his lifelong mentor Harvey Penick died. Crenshaw left Augusta with Kite to attend the funeral in their native Texas, only to return on the eve of the competition. In the interim, Crenshaw's game was transformed — magically — and he went on to capture The Masters against long odds. Afterward he said Harvey Penick's spirit was the 15th club in his bag, without which he could not have won.

The intangibles also are in place for Woods.

"He has the heart of a lion, it looks like," Tom Watson said. "He's a winner."

Courage and charisma, too. He is not afraid of the expectations.

"My goal is to be the best. I know that's a very lofty goal but if I try and don't [achieve it], I tried. I expect nothing but the best from myself."

When the final putt had fallen for par on the 18th hole, Woods hugged his caddie, Mike "Fluff" Cowan, and marched to the back of the final green. There he hugged his father, Earl — as both men fought back tears — and then hugged his mother, Kultida. More than anything else, Tiger said, the tears were joyous.

"More from relief. Every time I hug my Mom or Pop after a tournament, I know it's over. I know I accomplished my goal. To share it with them is something special.

"My dad said last night, 'If you play well and be yourself, it would be the most rewarding round you've ever had.'"

Moments later came the congratulatory phone call from President Bill Clinton, an avid golfer.

"He said the best shot he saw all week was the shot of me hugging my dad."

Proud papa Earl Woods said the victory hug is a family ritual. "No major is complete until we hug," Earl said. "I said, 'We did it. I love you and I'm so proud.'"

It was all but forgotten that Woods started the tournament shakily, with a 4-over-par 40 on the first nine holes. He played the final 63 holes in 22-under-par. He hit pitching wedge second shots into the 500-yard 15th hole, drove the ball an average of 323 yards in the tournament, and never hit more than a 7-iron into any par-4 all week. His putting was just as brilliant. Montgomerie said he was aware of Woods' ball-striking ability but was startled to see how well he could putt. On the treacherous Augusta greens, Woods did not three-putt in 72 holes.

Woods was determined not to lose his focus in the final round, no matter how large his lead grew.

"I knew I had to get through Amen Corner with par at the worst. I couldn't afford to let up on my concentration or anything. After I got by the water holes on the last nine, after I hit the tee shot at 16 — even though I screwed up and hit it to the right — I knew it was pretty much over because I knew I could bogey in. Those water holes, you know, can creep up and hurt you in a heartbeat.

"I knew I had to come out here and shoot a good score, execute and be patient, make birdies when I had a chance, which was probably the par-5s. I was able to do that, and I made birdies on 2, 8, and 13. And I only made two bogeys. That's how you win the last day.

"I never thought I would have the lead like I did. It's not what you envision. You envision dueling it out with, I guess, like, say, Faldo or Nicklaus or Watson, someone who's awfully tough to beat down the stretch. You dream of doing that or getting into a playoff, you know, weird things like that, but never to do it in the fashion that I did it. That's just something you never really dream of. It's just kind of nice that it actually became a reality.

"When I was 19, that's when I first played here, and I expected myself to win the tournament. And I just didn't and learned my lessons; came back the next year, learned my lessons; and this year it evolved into a victory. I grew up a lot playing my first major. I went through a lot of different things that week emotionally as far as things I had to deal with that I've never had to experience before. And I think that when I entered into a major, when I'm playing against the best players in the world and I saw the way they handled themselves and the way they conducted themselves, I learned and grew from that.

"I think I understand why the big guy up in the sky has given me some of these talents, and I think the main reason is to help people. I'm in a very unique position where a lot of kids look up to me just because I'm around their age group. They look up to me in a role model sense. And I think if I can influence their lives in a positive way, then I believe that's what the big guy in the sky had intended for me."

Woods, all aglow, didn't forget those who had gone before him — the African-American golfers who persevered against racism. He thanked them publicly. It was Lee Elder who broke the color barrier at The Masters in 1975. Elder literally raced to Augusta for the final round.

Elder, a member of the Senior PGA Tour, was home in Florida during Masters week and watched on television as Woods neared the historic moment. "I told my wife if he were anywhere near the lead, I was going to be there," Elder said. "This has more potential than Jackie Robinson breaking the color barrier in baseball." After Woods' Saturday round, Elder was so excited he couldn't sleep. He took a 7 A.M. flight to Atlanta but couldn't connect to Augusta. He rented a car for the 2½-hour drive. Halfway to Augusta, a Georgia state trooper clocked him doing 85 miles per hour in a 70-mile zone.

"I told him I have to get to The Masters to watch Tiger," Elder said. "He didn't know anything about golf."

When Elder finally arrived at Augusta National, where he played seven times in The Masters, the drive down Magnolia Lane gave him goosebumps. He was shaking all over. "It was wonderful," he said.

He visited briefly with Woods on the putting green before the final round.

"That meant a lot to me because he was the first, he was the one I looked up to. Because of what he did I was able to play on the PGA Tour. When Lee came down that really inspired me and reinforced what I had to do. I wasn't the pioneer. Charlie Sifford, Lee Elder, Ted Rhodes, those are the guys who paved the way. All night I was thinking about them, what they've done for me and the game of golf. Coming up 18, I said a little prayer of thanks to those guys. Those guys are the ones who did it."

One of the first questions asked Woods in the interview room afterward concerned the grand slam, a subject newspapers nationwide would flock to in the days ahead.

"Whether it's realistic or not, I couldn't really tell you, but I think it can be done. If you think about it, let's say, use for example, Phil Mickelson last year. I think he won four times. Well, if you win the right tournaments four times, then you have the slam.

"It's difficult to win because these are majors. These are the best players in the world under the most extreme conditions, circumstances. But I think you just peak at the right times — a lot like what Nicklaus used to do — if you can peak at the right times and have a lot of luck on your side. In order to win a big tournament, you've got to have a lot of luck. Then, who knows?"

The Celebrity Golfer

*T*iger Woods didn't return to the PGA Tour after The Masters for four weeks, but he was seldom out of the headlines or the lime-light.

There was a presidential snub, appearances on Oprah and Bar-bara Walters, openings of All-Star Cafes, a minivacation in Cancun, tabloid newspaper speculation about his love life, a hug from Sarah Ferguson, the Duchess of York, and, of course, the Fuzzy Zoeller incident.

On the Monday after his victory at Augusta National, President Bill Clinton invited Woods to join him at ceremonies honoring the 50th anniversary of Jackie Robinson's breaking baseball's color bar-rier. The festivities were at Shea Stadium in New York the next night, April 15. After all, Woods had spoken so eloquently at Augusta Na-tional about African-American golfers Charlie Sifford, Lee Elder, and Teddy Rhodes, men who had paved the way for him. Blacks were moved by Woods' candor and sincerity. Most golfers, black or white, could identify Sifford and Elder, but Rhodes was nearly unknown.

Rhodes, of Nashville, was "the black Bobby Jones" in the late 1940s. He won over 150 events on the United Golfers Association tour for black golfers and he won the National Negro Open four times. The mention of Rhodes stirred the emotions of many, among them Joe Hampton, Rhodes' lifelong friend. Hampton, 75, is the re-tired head professional at Ted Rhodes Golf Course in Nashville. Rhodes and Hampton were caddies together and golfing pals.

"You don't think that [Woods' comments] didn't bring some tears?" Hampton said. "We used to caddie at Belle Meade Country Club in Nashville. When the war broke out, we were separated. Ted went into the Navy; I went into the Army. He was discharged in Chi-cago and stayed around there, playing golf with Joe Louis, Billy Eckstein...he went all over the country playing golf. We had to make our own makeshift courses. There were no courses for us here in Nashville to play."

Rhodes, who died in 1969 at age 53, played in the Los Angeles Open and the Canadian Open before integration. The Cumberland golf course was renamed in his honor after his death. On April 10, the week Woods won The Masters, the clubhouse at Ted Rhodes was named after Hampton. Hampton had never met Tiger.

"My path has crossed all the black pros," Hampton said. "My path will cross with him sooner or later. It's been a great week around here."

President Clinton and his advisors no doubt felt Woods, still euphoric, would quickly accept the invitation to appear with him at Shea Stadium. The president offered to send an Air Force jet for Woods.

Sorry, Tiger said. Busy. Things to do, places to go. There was the grand opening of All-Star Cafes in Myrtle Beach, South Carolina — golf country — and Atlantic City. The schedule had forced him a couple of weeks earlier to cancel an appearance at Darius Rucker's charity event in South Carolina, just 80 miles up the road from Augusta National, the day after The Masters. Of course, that would be Darius Rucker of Hootie and the Blowfish, so that also made Woods the master of one-upmanship — blowing off Hootie and the Blowfish.

By Tuesday night, Woods would be lounging on a hotel balcony in Cancun, Mexico. Woods declined the Presidential offer, politely but firmly. A White House spokesperson said the President did not take it as a snub. Others didn't agree. They saw it quite differently. Noted columnist Maureen Dowd, writing in the *New York Times* later in the week, said, "...as snubs go, this one was pretty impressive." Dowd also quoted author/writer/authority John Feinstein: "I guess (Woods) feels, with some justification, that right now he's bulletproof." Dowd continued, suggesting the snub was a payback, an in-your-face to the President for when Clinton wound up in a golf game with Greg Norman instead of Tiger Woods the year before.

Why Clinton — or anybody else for that matter — would choose Norman over Woods is the mystery. As Colin Montgomerie put it so succinctly after the third round of The Masters at Augusta National, Greg Norman is not Tiger Woods.

But who exactly is Tiger Woods?

Tiger stirred up another controversy a week later when he appeared on "The Oprah Winfrey Show" that aired April 24. Woods discussed The Masters, his meteoric rise as a professional golfer and celebrity, and many other subjects. But when it was over, people were talking about only one topic — the word coined by Woods to reflect his heritage. Cablinasian. Some were offended, others were pleased.

The derivation of the word is a blending of Woods' ethnic heritage — Caucasian, Black, Indian, and Asian. He is one-fourth black, Thai, and Chinese; one-eighth white and one-eighth American Indian. As a youth, Woods, unsure of how to describe his ethnicity, always ticked off two boxes on personal forms — African-American and Asian.

Woods, a Buddhist, defended his usage of the term Cablinasian in an interview with Barbara Walters on ABC and insisted he wasn't denying his black heritage.

"I'm not doing that at all. If I said I was strictly African-American, that's saying my mom never existed and that's wrong. I love my mom to death. That's my little mommy."

Woods told Walters his first racial incident occurred when he was five. His first day at kindergarten, he was tied to a tree by the older kids. The abuse did not stop there. The word "nigger" was written on him.

"I had rocks thrown at me. I was bleeding all over the place and went home."

Many years later, after his triumph at Augusta National, there was another racial incident. Perhaps it wasn't mean-spirited — Fuzzy Zoeller isn't a mean person — but there were serious repercussions.

As Zoeller walked off the 18th green on the final day of The Masters, he was trailed by a small group of media. He answered a couple of harmless questions before somebody finally got around to asking about the young man who was bound for glory that afternoon. "Well done," Zoeller said, and all the other right things. Then he did something lawyers learn in Law School 101 and witnesses are told in the first briefing before trial. Answer the question directly. Do not annotate. When the answer is complete, stop. But Fuzzy is Fuzzy. He's affable, a great quote, and demonstrative, all the way back to the 1984 U.S. Open at Winged Foot, where he waved the white towel of surrender to Greg Norman. Zoeller was baiting a shark trap back then. He caught up to Norman and beat him in a play-off. At Augusta National, the only person to get snared was Zoeller.

Zoeller answered the questions and kept talking. Big mistake.

"That little boy is driving well and he's putting well," Zoeller said with a CNN camera nearby. "He's doing everything it takes to win. So, you know what you guys do when he gets in here? You pat him on the back and say congratulations and enjoy it and tell him not to serve fried chicken next year. Got it?"

Zoeller snapped his fingers, turned to walk away, and then added, "Or collard greens or whatever the hell they serve."

The Masters winner selects the menu for the champions' dinner on the eve of the next tournament. The menus are usually regional. For example, Sandy Lyle's choice featured a dish native to Scotland — haggis — which is the minced heart, lungs, and liver of a sheep or calf mixed with suet, oatmeal, and seasonings, and boiled in the stomach of the animal. Woods' romp had the press room pundits speculating on his choice of dishes and the consensus was that the likely choice would be Tiger's favorite repast — fast-food burger and fries. Zoeller, a 24-year veteran of the PGA Tour, is a past winner at The Masters. He won in his first appearance at Augusta National in 1979.

Once the story broke on CNN's "Pro Golf Weekly" show, the rebuke was swift and forceful. Kmart, which had an endorsement deal with Zoeller and carried golf equipment with his name and likeness, deemed the comments racially insensitive, offensive, and inappropriate. Kmart had sponsored Zoeller for six years, but the company immediately canceled the contract, which had 20 months left. The company's press release said Zoeller's comments were "contrary to Kmart's longstanding policies that ensure our words and deeds are without bias."

Two days before the Greater Greensboro Open, Zoeller withdrew from the event, saying he couldn't and wouldn't play again on the PGA Tour until he made things straight with Woods. Zoeller was under intense pressure and the African-American community was threatening to picket and boycott the tournament. The local NAACP chapter demanded, and accepted, a further apology from Zoeller, but he couldn't take much more.

Choking back tears, Zoeller said his respect for the game of golf dictated his withdrawal. "It hurts," he said. "I am the one who screwed up and I will pay the price. I started this, and I feel strongly that I have to make things right with Tiger first before anything else. I also regret the distraction this has caused the world of golf. What I said is distracting people at this tournament. And that's not fair to the other people on this course trying to play this tournament."

Woods, by this time distanced from the golf community during an extended break in his playing schedule, was stunned by Zoeller's remarks, and it took him several days to respond. He said he was in important meetings with Nike executives and couldn't break away to return Zoeller's calls. When he did, it was in the form of a statement released by his management group, International Management Group of Cleveland.

"At first, I was shocked to hear that Fuzzy Zoeller made these unfortunate remarks," the statement read. "His attempt at humor was out-of-bounds, and I was disappointed by it. But having played golf with Fuzzy, I know he is a jokester; and I have concluded that no personal animosity toward me was intended.

"I respect Fuzzy as a golfer and as a person, and for the many good things he has done for others throughout his career. I know he feels badly about the remarks. We all make mistakes, and it is time to move on. I accept Fuzzy's apology and hope everyone can now put this behind us."

But there were golfers on the PGA Tour who were furious with Woods for allowing Zoeller to hang. They wondered, as did the general public, how long the affair would have been allowed to linger had Zoeller, like Woods, been represented by IMG. (Zoeller is represented by Eddie Elias Enterprises, Inc.) The answer was obvious — not long. Or, perhaps not at all.

The fallout continued for weeks, even months, and left PGA Tour members wary of discussing Woods with the media. They either declined entirely to do so — at one point, Nick Faldo responded to an inquiry with, "No — not now, not ever" — or sugar-coated comments until they were worthless blather. For that, they could not be condemned.

May

He's Back

Tiger Woods never missed a beat in his return to the PGA Tour. He won the $1.8 million GTE Byron Nelson Classic by two strokes, his fifth victory in 16 starts on the PGA Tour — the third of 1997 and the second in successive starts. He won despite not having his 'A' game, a subject that would be the source of some controversy in the weeks to come. Afterward, there was a hug from Sarah Ferguson, the Duchess of York.

"Sarah and I are good friends. We've talked a lot [on the telephone]."

Woods met the Duchess "through Kevin." Of course, that would be Kevin Costner, actor and pro-am partner.

The pre-tournament press debriefing was the longest and most thorough anybody could remember. The transcripts filled 40 pages and touched on every topic imaginable, and even some that weren't. There are cases in front of the Supreme Court that didn't require such lengthy transcripts or so many questions.

Mr. Woods, do you swear to tell the truth, the whole truth and nothing but the truth — so help you God?

Let's begin.

Tiger, what have these last four weeks been like for you, hanging out with rock stars and Michael Jordan?

"A lot of it has been actually a lot of work as far as business, taking care of all the sponsorships...I'm engaged in right now. Business meeting after business meeting after business meeting. Basically just getting involved with what's going on and getting caught up on all the details."

Are you anxious to get back in competition?

"I really am. I wanted to come back a little earlier, possibly play either last week or Houston. But my body kept telling me 'no.' I needed some more time off; I needed to rest. My mind wasn't exactly ready to go yet, but now it is."

What are your expectations this week?

"I came here to win."

Is there a chance you'll play another sport? It's fashionable to do that.

"Is sleeping a sport?"

After winning the Masters have there been an awful lot of demands on your time?

"You would not believe. I mean, the demands on my time have grown exponentially. It's been amazing. I've had to learn the magic word 'no' and to say it as nice as possible. But it's hard because people still, I think, in my opinion fail to realize why I'm out here. I'm out here to try and win tournaments, and sometimes they want me to either schmooze with these people, do interviews, sign tons of autographs, take pictures with their kids. That's great and all, but I can't lose sight of my main objective, my main focus, which is winning."

What do you love about golf?

"Competing."

Regarding the controversy with Fuzzy Zoeller, if you had to do it over again would you do anything differently?

"I think I handled the situation appropriately. To be honest with you, I didn't want to even issue a statement because I didn't do any-

thing wrong. That was my concern. And I was drawn into a situation where I had no choice but to do that. I think I responded appropriately with the statement. I look at it this way: I didn't dig myself into the hole, but I got drawn into it. Now it's over, and we can all move on."

What do you think of Byron Nelson's 11 straight victories?

"I don't think that will ever be done again."

A lot of people were surprised that you declined an invitation from President Clinton to attend the Jackie Robinson ceremony.

"One, I had planned my vacation already. It was set. And, two, why didn't Mr. Clinton invite me before the Masters? That didn't happen. And as soon as I won, he invited me. If he wanted me there, I think it would have been best if he would have [asked] before, with all the other athletes that were involved."

What advice did Michael Jordan give you?

"We've talked a lot lately, and he's given me some great advice and I've bounced some stuff off him, what I thought. And I think the one comment that, whether it's Kevin or Mike or Charles [Barkley] or anyone I talked to, I think what they all say, you're going to have to find your own way, your own path of what works best for you. Because only you know. We can only sit here and tell you what we think, what's worked best for us. And it's going to take time. And in the meantime you're doing great and keep it up."

After that cross-examination, the golf tournament was a piece of cake. Woods played like he had never been away. "That's what happens when you're a Cadillac," Paul Stankowski said. "All it takes is a little fine tuning. Now, us old Volkswagens, we take some time to get warmed up."

Woods opened with a pair of 64s, which tied him with Lee Rinker for the lead after 36 holes. Rinker, who was giving competitive golf another try after a couple of years behind the pro shop counter, shot a second-round 63. Woods' 67 gave him a 2-shot lead over five golfers but he was so displeased with his ball-striking that he sent out a

Mayday call to his teacher, Butch Harmon, who made the four-hour drive from Houston and joined Woods on the practice tee early Sunday morning for a sprucing up session. What happened next isn't a surprise. Even casual observers and novices knew that Woods vs. Rinker was a mismatch, and that proved to be the case. Woods finally applied the clincher when he hit driver-driver on the par 5 16th hole, chipped to within a few feet, and knocked in the birdie putt to close things out.

"I hit some really good shots and some really bad shots. I had to rely on my mind and my short game to get me through, and that's what happened. I got up and down every time. Winning like this means a lot. You're not always going to have your 'A' game, or close to it."

Woods gave himself a "C+."

Chillin'

Golf's hottest player got a "frosty" reception in Fort Worth.

The showdown at the MasterCard Colonial in Fort Worth was another mismatch on paper. In this corner, phenom Tiger Woods, seeking a third straight victory. In that corner, David Ogrin, the man with an unorthodox swing who has been a bit player on the PGA Tour for 15 years. Ogrin finally broke through for his first victory after 405 tournaments at the 1996 LaCantera Texas Open in San Antonio. That was exactly one week after Woods, playing in his fifth PGA Tour event as a professional, won for the first time. Ogrin already had a taste of what it's like with a Tiger on your tail at LaCantera, where Woods rallied with a final-round 67 to finish third, two strokes behind the winner.

Ogrin catapulted into the lead with a third-round 62 but he couldn't shake Woods, who matched him nearly stroke for stroke with a haughty little 64 of his own. Ogrin's 196, 14 under par, was two shots better than Tiger. Ogrin had the LaCantera Open to fall back on if he needed to bolster his mind-set for the coming battle. "That was before the hurricane of Tigermania hit," said Ogrin, who made six birdies in a row. "I'm looking forward to playing him. You've got to want to face Michael Jordan — to go up against the best."

But Woods wasn't the best player in the field in the final round. That distinction belonged to South African David Frost, whose plodding paid off with a 3-under-par 67, which enabled him to rally from a three-shot deficit for his 10th Tour victory. Ogrin and Brad Faxon were two shots behind, and Woods, after 72, tied for fourth.

Woods' round unraveled with two double bogeys.

"I didn't play well. I was hitting a lot of long iron shots over the green, and then I finally hit one short on No. 9 where there was water. It was just some mechanical problems. I've had them all week, and they finally caught up with me."

Frost charged into the lead with a 25-foot birdie putt at the 17th hole. Moments later, the same hole would be Woods' final undoing. He missed the green long with a pitching wedge, starting a sequence that led to his second double bogey.

It was Ogrin — not Frost or Woods — who put the scenario into focus.

"This was mine for a while to win or lose," Ogrin said. "But my putter was not working. It became a foreign object the last nine holes. It was pressure that caused that. I had some things riding on it. Playing in the eye of a hurricane was fine. It's like being in surround-sound at a movie."

There was a lot going on at the Colonial. On Monday, Woods and American Express announced an endorsement deal reported to be $13 million. How's that for in-your-face golf — American Express stealing the thunder from credit card rival MasterCard at its own tournament. On Tuesday, he finally had his man-to-man with Fuzzy Zoeller. "I explained to him how it happened and that I meant nothing by it," Zoeller said. Woods concurred.

"We had a nice talk. I found out some things I needed to know. I let him know how I felt. Now it's over. The incident is one of many that's going to happen over my career. I've had a lot worse than this. Hopefully, I won't have a situation like this ever again, but it's probably unlikely."

For comic relief, there was Ogrin. He was in the interview room after his 62 in Round III when Woods arrived. "No three-peat for that guy," Ogrin said. "Uh-uh. Not." It was all Woods could do to keep from laughing.

Faxon, one of the most affable guys on Tour, challenged with a final round 68 to grab a share of second place with Ogrin. He used the forum to make a point. "I didn't have my 'A' game today. It was C-minus. I'm flying my coaches in tomorrow," said Faxon, who had advised Woods earlier about the pitfalls of such pronouncements. Golf professionals don't like to be beaten by somebody's C-game. It's embarrassing to begin with, and an insult when the matter is publicized. "If he wants people to like him out here, he's got to watch it," Faxon said. "He's a good guy, a sensitive enough guy. You don't want to ostracize yourself. He's going to be around a long time. I want to get along with him. I think everybody does."

"Nobody ever said anything to me, except Brad. All I'm doing is telling the truth. You ask a question and I'll tell you straight out. Look at the way I played at Augusta. It was pretty good. Now it's a lot different."

Woods' relationship toward others on Tour already was being called standoffish. It became downright thorny when it was revealed that Woods had declined to autograph a ball for Billy Andrade, a New Englander who — along with Brad Faxon — supports a tournament called Charities for Children. Woods told Faxon he doesn't sign golf balls. The Woods ball would have joined a collection with every living Masters champion, which was eventually auctioned to benefit the charity. Faxon and Davis Love III, a member of the PGA Tour Policy Board, met with Woods the next day. "Tiger just needs some friends out here to tell him what's going on — things nobody else would tell him," Love said.

Jack's Tournament

Memorial Tournament
Muirfield Village Golf Club
Dublin, Ohio
May 29–June 1

*T*iger Woods didn't play well at the Memorial Tournament, but he made the cut. For that, he could thank Fuzzy Zoeller. How's that for a scene-setter?

But Woods' shortcomings in Ohio didn't silence the speculation about the Grand Slam. By midweek, that's all anybody was talking about or writing about — Woods' pursuit of golf's Impregnable Quadrilateral.

Woods opened with 72 and the first question during his post-round scrum with reporters was: "How would you grade your play today?"

"I don't do that anymore."

Once again, the Memorial — Jack Nicklaus' tournament on a course he designed — was beset by foul weather, but there was plenty going on. As in every Tour stop, the local media was waiting for Woods with bated breath. Not all media are the same. There are two kinds of reporters covering the PGA Tour. There are the "beat" people — golf writers who travel with the Tour, get to know the players, and stay up with all the developments. Those include both print and electronic media. Then there are the local media sent out by assignment editors. Their knowledge of golf — or any story, for that matter — is likely to be minimal. They have instructions from above on what questions to ask, no matter how silly they might be, and always look for a local angle. They ask questions like "How would you grade your play today?" without realizing its implications. Or, "How do you like Ohio?" Meanwhile, the golf writers try hard to get the press conference back on track with questions related to the game and, in this case, Woods' chances for a grand slam with the U.S. Open just around the corner.

Question: Do you feel like you're kind of at home because of the International Management Group connection out of Cleveland?
Answer: *This isn't Cleveland.*
Question: Ohio.
Answer: *No.*
Question: You don't?
Answer: *No.*

Later,

Question: Tiger, I want to ask you about the fans. Is there anything that stands out about central Ohio, about the people here?
Answer: *I've been here 20 minutes.*

Once past the comic relief, the press conference at Muirfield Village touched on some important subjects, among them the lifestyle of a megastar. The pace is frenetic. There is nothing routine anymore, and Woods made the point that his religion, Buddhism, helped to guide him through the tumult. The string bracelet he wears on his left wrist is a Buddhist symbol for strength and protection. The ultimate state of Buddhism is Nirvana, or enlightenment. Woods was becoming wiser each day, and he was better able to reconcile his celebrity status with reality. He still had to do some things normally associated with mere mortals. Like grocery shopping.

"I still get hungry.
"Sometimes, just to be able to go to a grocery store and not be bugged for a photo or asked for autographs and stuff, that sometimes can wear on you; or at dinner when you've got food in your mouth and people are coming up to you and want to take a picture and ask

for an autograph, too. That part of my old life I do miss, but I've accepted it, too."

Woods has made few concessions to stardom. There were few trappings, save for a new car, a Mercedes. It requires gas — and that requires the art of signing autographs. A stop for gas without autograph seekers is a rare event. There are few places Woods can go without being spotted.

"Let's see, the last [gas stop] there were five [autograph requests]. I can tell you this: I have adjusted to everything and I've accepted a lot of things that now come with being who I am. Before The Masters, I was kind of struggling with it, but I think that month off really did help out a lot."

There is no precedent to Tigermania. The media glare didn't blind a young Arnold Palmer, and Jack Nicklaus wasn't a fan favorite until after the King abdicated. Bobby Jones, the legendary amateur, was feted with two ticker-tape parades in New York City, but the levels of exposure in the 1920s and 1930s were not atomic. "It's a frenzy — and it's wonderful," Tom Watson said. "But for the person who's in the center of this, he needs some buffer. I don't see anything stopping him. The only thing I think would stop him would be he'll start hating the zoo — the frenzy — he'll want to get away from it in the worst way. He's a phenomenon is what he is. Right now, Tiger is the man."

Woods, like all great champions, is driven. His goals were defined many years ago, as a youth, and they included taping a list of Nicklaus' achievements on a wall in his bedroom as motivation. Now he was at Muirfield, Jack's course, playing in Jack's tournament. The media numbers were enormous — at least 18 television cameras and dozens of photographs at the Woods press conference, with a huge Japanese contingent giving the setting an international flair.

When Nicklaus arrived for his pre-tournament State of the Memorial address, it didn't take long for the discussion to move toward Woods and the possibility of a grand slam. The modern Grand Slam — the Masters, the U.S. Open, the British Open, and the PGA Championship — has never been achieved in the same year. But

Woods' dominating performance at Augusta had a lot of people who know the game and its history suggesting that he had a chance, even as a 21-year-old. Nicklaus' response was diplomatic. "I think anybody winning all four is a very, very difficult chore," he said. "But it's possible."

Nicklaus' decision to turn pro was based not on dollars but on "wanting to be the best golfer I could be, play against the best competition. That's the only way you could do it, was play against the best."

"I don't think the money will make a difference to this kid," he said. "But the frenzy around him is hard. I'm really quite interested in seeing what's going to happen to him. Every single thing he's going to do will be right in your newspapers. It will be under a microscope. It's a tough way to live. But I think he's quite capable of doing it."

The Memorial Tournament also marked John Daly's return to the PGA Tour. Daly withdrew from The Players Championship in March after going on a night-long drinking binge — followed by an incident at a Ponte Vedra Beach hotel — and entered a rehabilitation facility in California to deal with his alcohol-related problems. His return wasn't victorious. It was cautious and hopeful.

"I don't have any expectations this week, just getting back into the rhythm, the basics of my game," Daly said. "More importantly, I didn't get to play a lot of golf while I was gone. I was working on more important things. But I'm excited. I have faith in the equipment I'm using and I'm really excited to get it going."

The new equipment company was Callaway Golf, which stepped in after Wilson — which had a much-publicized multimillion-dollar contract with Daly — finally had had enough and dropped him. Daly insisted this time would be different and recited scriptures from the Alcoholics Anonymous bible. He received hundreds of letters during his absence. "There's about 1,800 more I haven't opened," he said. "I just couldn't get all the way through them in the six weeks that I was there. It may take me forever to go through all that. But it made me realize that I'm not alone, that there's other people out there just like myself that have this same disease, and it's a tough battle." In the next few weeks Daly would find that it wasn't over yet.

On Monday before the Memorial Tournament, Woods and Daly attracted a crowd of about 30,000 at the third annual Mystic Rock Charity Pro-Am in Farmington, Pennsylvania, to benefit children's leukemia research. Woods treated them to a 7-under 65, Daly a "rusty" 1-over 73. It was a different Woods than people see in a Tour event. He was signing autographs on the tees, chatting it up and smiling. Woods, according to published reports, was being paid $1 million to appear at Joe Hardy's outing for three years. Hardy, a multimillionaire lumberman, founded the Nemacolin Woodlands Resort and hopes the pro-am is a forerunner of a PGA Tour stop at the Pete Dye-designed course.

"Going back to when I was a child, I used to go down to a children's hospital and speak to cancer patients as well as abused kids. It's something I liked to do — loved to do. Any time I can give something back, I'm more than happy to."

Woods greeted Daly's return warmly.

"I think it's great for the game. I think it's great for society to see that a guy has enough guts to admit that he has a problem and to go get it taken care of. That's not easy to do. I admire him for that."

Daly and his mentor, Zoeller, played a practice round at Muirfield Village two days later. Daly's new black Callaway bag was in stark contrast to the plain bag Zoeller was using since his deal with Kmart was terminated over the Woods controversy. Zoeller hit his tee ball down the middle of the fairway, turned to Daly, and said, "Take that, Big Boy. After what I've been through the last three weeks I ain't afraid of you."

Tim "Lumpy" Herron was among the first-round leaders with 66. He was no stranger to Muirfield Village or to Woods. Herron and Woods were matched at the 1992 U.S. Amateur, which was played on the Nicklaus design. Herron, 22 at the time, was an All-America golfer at New Mexico who drew the U.S. Junior Amateur champion.

"I don't remember much about it," Herron said. "I remember getting up and down on the first hole and that's about it. I just remember I kept the ball in play and that I wasn't going to let up because all the college guys were heckling me on the range. They were saying they wouldn't want to play him and get beat by a 15-year-old."

Herron won, 6-and-4, but two years later, in 1994, Woods began a stretch of three straight victories in the U.S. Amateur.

"I felt like he was going to be special," Herron said. "But you never know when a kid is going to burn out. You really don't have a clue. I remember a guy from *USA Today* asked me, 'When should he turn pro?' I said, 'I just beat him. I don't think he should turn pro right now.' But I did think he did everything at the right time. He's done everything right, and I'm glad I'm in his era. I think he's only going to do good for the game and that he's going to put more money in our pockets, too, so it works out well.

"Just don't steal all the majors from us."

There was never a threat that Woods would steal the Memorial Tournament.

His 72-75 start barely enabled him to make the cut, and that only because of Zoeller's generosity.

Zoeller had a 12-foot birdie putt on the final hole of the second round that would have moved the cut to 146. He left it just short, in the heart, and Woods' streak of cuts — now 20 — was intact. Zoeller's miss also allowed Daly to slip into the weekend, where he was paired with Woods.

"My swing is really not there. This course beat me up. I just had some bad shots and made some mental mistakes."

But the world did learn something at the Memorial Tournament about Woods' swing. Most golf professionals say they swing well within themselves, at perhaps 75 percent or 80 percent of their capacity. However, Woods' swing is so powerful, so forceful, that it looks like he's swinging 115 percent every time. How hard does he swing exactly?

"About 80, max. People don't realize I've got another 30 yards on my game if I want it. It's not that hard for me. It's like Nolan Ryan throwing a fast ball that goes only 90 miles an hour. He's just cruising and that's about what I'm doing. See, the thing is, I can hit it 30

yards farther, but I give up so much accuracy that way so I never do it. There are certain times I can go ahead and dig down deep and hit it farther."

With the spotlight off Woods for a change, it was now on the weather and the never-ending rainshowers. Scott Hoch surged into the second-round lead, followed a shot behind by Vijay Singh. The conditions provided plenty of clues to the outcome — if anybody was going to be Singh-ing in the rain, it would be Vijay.

The third round couldn't be completed Sunday, so those who made the cut were back again Monday. Singh returned to the middle of the 11th fairway to execute his second shot on the par 5 hole, a shot he couldn't possibly have played the day before because of the condition of the course when the siren suspended play.

He sent a towering 3-wood shot toward the pin 247 yards away, on an elevated green set just beyond a creek. The ball finished 18 inches from the cup for a tap-in eagle. That's all Singh needed. He closed with a 67 for a 54-hole 202 total, ahead of runners-up Jim Furyk and Greg Norman.

June

The U.S. Open

The U.S. Open Championship
Congressional Country Club
Bethesda, Maryland
June 12–15

The U.S. Open at Congressional Country Club, where presidents and lawmakers play golf, was a historic four-man showdown. Tiger Woods wasn't in the contending four-ball, and talk of a Grand Slam died an inglorious death for 1997. All the things people were saying about the difficulty and difference of a U.S. Open, as compared to The Masters, proved to be true. Typically, Woods never quite went away. He was always lurking, always threatening to make a move despite a poor start. But it didn't quite happen. Congressional and its U.S. Open setup got the best of him, and Tiger didn't mind saying so. He shot 74-67-73-72—286 to tie for 19th, 10 shots behind champion Ernie Els.

"I'm glad the suffering is over. This course wore me out. I hit some good shots, and I hit some bad shots. And it took its toll on me. It humbled me. It humbled me big-time and that's just the way it is. In the U.S. Open, it's going to humble you whether you want it to or not, because the demands of a U.S. Open are so tough and so strenuous that you're going to get worn out.

"It's a typical U.S. Open. You know that you're going to go out there and face holes where you're going to have a good tee shot and a good second shot. You have to hit two good shots in a row — not like a par 5, where I can kind of cheat with a driver and an iron."

Woods was hitting all kinds of uncharacteristic shots and, more alarmingly, he was three-putting, something he didn't do in 72 holes at Augusta National. At Congressional, he three-putted eight times. He insisted he wasn't pressing, trying to make something happen, or letting the Grand Slam talk get in his way. It was simply a matter of not having control of his golf game. He could never get on a roll and he couldn't attack the course.

Those are the two things that separate Woods. He's a momentum player. Once he gets on a roll, it's an awesome sight: the red numbers drip from the leaderboard like raindrops in San Francisco. When he gets on those rolls, he reduces a golf course to nothing, like Nicklaus had said at Augusta National. But the U.S. Open demands greater patience and a more conservative approach. Woods tried to alter his mindset. That wasn't the problem. He was geared to play more cautiously.

"I'd love to have made 72 straight pars and see what my chances were. That's just the way the U.S. Open is and I knew that going in. Unfortunately, I didn't hit it good, I didn't putt well. Overall, it was a good week. I did have some fun. I learned a lot. The details of it I'm not going to explain to you, because I think that's private. I will tell you this: I did make some mental mistakes out there that I will rectify so I'll never make them again.

"It was a grind. My mind was tested and my patience, my grit, every kind of emotion you can conjure up was tested this week. And, I think I held up pretty good. Could have held up better."

President Clinton and his daughter Chelsea — who was Stanford-bound in the fall — watched the final round from the 16th fairway. Woods birdied the hole, hitting a 6-iron in from 196 yards and making the putt, which had a three-foot right-to-left break. Woods said he wasn't aware the President and Chelsea were in his gallery.

"That's great. It's the only putt I made all week."

Again, Woods was asked to grade his game at the U.S. Open.

"I'm not doing that anymore. I told you guys that at Colonial."

Nobody had to ask Ernie Els to grade his performance at Congressional. It was A-plus. In a four-way battle with Americans Tom

Lehman and Jeff Maggert and Scotland's Colin Montgomerie — the first-day leader — Els was picture perfect. It was the second U.S. Open crown in four years for the 27-year-old South African. Els also won at Oakmont Country Club, outside of Pittsburgh, in 1994, where he beat Montgomerie and Loren Roberts in a 20-hole play-off.

Els is unflappable, with a long, flowing swing that has so much rhythm that lyrics should be added. Lehman started the final round with a two-shot lead, but by the 11th hole all four golfers were tied at 4 under par. Only Els could stay there. First Maggert, then Lehman and Montgomerie — both at the 17th hole — lost their share of the lead. "Funny things happen in majors," Els said. "You've just got to hang in there. At U.S. Opens, you just try to make par." Right, and Woods would have taken 72 of them.

Lehman, who was in the final group at the U.S. Open for the third straight year, watched his chances disappear into a pond left of the 17th green. His second shot, a 7-iron with his bread-and-butter draw shape, came up just short and landed in the water. "I'd give anything in the world for a mulligan," Lehman said. "It was a shock to look up and see the ball not going where I wanted it to go."

There had been a lot of talk about rivalries, and a rival for Woods. Palmer had Nicklaus, Nicklaus had Watson, Hogan had Snead, and now Woods needed somebody to challenge him and push him to greater heights. Els was on the short list of those prominently mentioned — along with Phil Mickelson and John Daly — and with one major victory each in 1997, the Woods–Els rivalry was beginning to shape up. The contrasts, of course, were the stuff of a Hollywood script. A blonde from South Africa, a nation which until recently had practiced apartheid, and a Cablinasian kid from California with his mixed ethnic and racial heritage.

"Well, if my outside is very calm, I think inside any player will tell you that you're pretty intense and tense," Els said. "I was quite intense. But I had confidence in myself and I had confidence in my game. Other times, it might be different. I felt comfortable. I think, with experience, you become a little bit more calm. You have to be calm to win major tournaments. There's a very big spotlight on golf at the moment with the emergence of Tiger Woods and other really good players. So it seems like there's more attention and there's a lot more pressure, I think, even from the time when I won in '94.

"You're going to a different class now. A lot of guys have won one major. I've won two. You don't want to get too far ahead of yourself, but I'm very happy at the moment. Obviously, there's a lot of young players in their 20s coming through and golf is very healthy at the moment. It's a great feeling to win two before you are 30. I think John Daly was the last guy to do it and I'm sure Tiger will probably win a couple before he's 25. But at least I've got two now and I'm looking for more."

Els became the first foreign player since Alex Smith of Scotland to win a pair of U.S. Opens. Smith did it in 1906 and 1910. The Open was a battle of attrition. Rains interrupted and suspended play Friday and Saturday and caused lengthy delays. The most damaging sequence for Woods came in the third round when, in the fading light of dusk, he made four bogeys in five holes.

With the rain delays, it took him more than six hours to complete the round. Still, there was some magic. At the 11th hole, Woods hit an errant approach shot that caromed off the grandstands into a greenside swale, 55 feet from the flagstick. For mortals, it was a lumpy putt or a bump-and-run or maybe a lob. For Woods, it was one of those creative shots — a chip with a 3-wood that went up a hill, over a ridge, and into the cup. It moved him to one under for the day and lurking once again. Scott Dunlap, Woods' little-known playing partner, watched the shot with admiration. "There's nothing wrong with his game," Dunlap said. "Other than the best player doesn't win all the time." Woods made bogey out of a bunker on the 12th, then three-putted the 13th, 14th, and 16th holes — the last from only about 15 feet. At the 16th, the siren halting play sounded at 8:20 P.M. just as Woods — practically in the dark — was sizing up the first putt. He had the option of completing the hole or marking his ball and hitting the putt upon the resumption of play the next morning.

"Oh, man, I putted horrible this week. My speed was off, and when your speed is off on greens this fast with this much slope, your

line's going to be off and fluctuating. I had a tough time hitting my line because my speed was bad. And I just need to work on my mechanics and hopefully a better feel. If I would have putted well, I probably would have shot anywhere near even par."

That's the kind of week it was for Woods. He wasn't alone. Greg Norman missed the cut, making it the first time in his career he'd miss advancing in both The Masters and the U.S. Open in the same year. But Norman, like Woods, was busy off the course. Norman bought a $30 million Boeing 737 and announced an agreement to be an ambassador for Boeing Business Jets.

Not far away, in downtown Washington, DC, Nike unveiled the new Tiger logo and clothes line. The oval-shaped Tiger logo was inspired, according to Gordon Thompson, Nike's vice president of design, by Woods' heritage and his personality. The design features two-directional arrows symbolizing many things, according to Thompson. "The oval shape is symbolic of both the globe and the golf swing plane," he said. "Within the oval are the arrows — which are balanced, yet dynamic in that space — representing Tiger's focused yet passionate style of play. The overall look is balance and unity between opposing forces." The logo is red, black, and white — red for Tiger's victory color. The red and black together represent his Asian/African heritage.

According to Kultida Woods, red is Tiger's power color, and he wears it on Sundays. The result is Tiger Sunday — his wardrobe for the final round — which consists of a red shirt and black slacks. The new apparel highlights those colors, but with a slightly different look.

Daly's appearance at the U.S. Open was short-lived, but even in a relatively short period Big John made his presence felt. Daly never made it to the 10th tee Friday. He shot 77 in the opening round, played nine holes Friday, and then left playing partners Els and Payne Stewart waiting on the 10th tee.

Woods had been kicked off the back nine at Congressional two days earlier during a practice round. At 7:45 A.M., Woods, playing alone, was told by a United States Golf Association official that he could not continue because he had not been given permission to go out on the back nine. Here's the tie-in to Daly: Woods and Daly had signed up to play a practice round in the afternoon. Daly invited his buddy, Fuzzy Zoeller, to join them, and the time was changed to 7:50 A.M. When Woods discovered he would have another playing partner, Zoeller, he went off by himself on the back nine. But in doing so he ran afoul of the USGA. The USGA and grounds crews begin setting up the course each morning before dawn, and nobody is allowed out until maintenance is completed. Woods said he wanted to play early to avoid the crowds, which were substantial at Congressional and always in search of Woods. He never mentioned Zoeller.

While Woods' 74 bettered Daly's first round by 3 shots, his mood was no more congenial. Woods got it to 2 under early but played the back nine like a high handicapper, 6 over for the last eight, including a double bogey 5 at the controversial par 3 finishing hole where he hit his tee shot into the water. He couldn't help but think...

"I've had some disappointing rounds lately and this is one of them."

The wet ball at the 18th turned out to be prophetic. He had been asked about it before the tournament.

"It's not the traps you're worried about. It's that H_2O stuff."

When Woods came off the course, he hurried past reporters, declining to comment. The USGA media staff had to track him down, along with a couple of pool reporters, for a few terse comments. What was on Tiger's mind?

"You don't want to know."

But there was plenty to be learned at Congressional. Woods was funny and candid with many of his responses. For example, there is a 13-year-old in New Zealand who fancies himself a Tiger disciple. The lad is called Leopard Lee and he dominates all the junior golf in his country. Asked what advice he would have for the youngster, Woods said his parents should not push him.

"I hope he is the type of person who is very self-driven, self-motivated, because this is the kind of game you can't really rely on a

coach or anyone to do it for you. You have to go out there and push yourself to be the best. And, I'm sure he'll get out here and he'll be kicking my butt."

On being a role model:

"It's an honor. It really is. I'm in a position where I can help out people in a positive way, and what more do you want? I mean, that's perfect. I can influence kids in a good way. And, I try. I try and do my best. The foundation I've set up trying to help kids in the inner city and then teach them there's another sport out here besides your core sports in America. I think that's so important that you give kids hope. I think by being a positive role model, I think you can do that. Because when I was a little boy I had my father as well as a couple of other people. They were my role models. If people have positive role models, they'll be positive people."

On his father's experience as a military man:

"The biggest lesson he's taught me that's helped me out here is probably the psychological warfare that he had to endure being a Green Beret...dealing with a lot of adversity and how to go through that. It's this method he's taught me and it's worked pretty good. And I've had to deal with a lot of things as I've turned pro. And I've noticed that once I start playing in a tournament, I'm fine. All the things my dad has taught me, it definitely is working."

Finally, on admonishing golf crowds to behave properly:

"I wish I could. But if I say something like that, I might be looked at as a bad guy. What we want to do is bring a lot of people into the game. You have to understand, these people are coming to a game they don't know. It would be like me going to watch cricket. I don't know a whole lot about cricket. I might sit there and cheer at the wrong time. As people go to tournaments and experience them and learn and then also talk to people who do play golf, their behavior is obviously going to improve and they're going to understand. It's going to take some time, though."

There is a sidebar to Woods' third-round 73, which left him at 214 after 54 holes. Woods finished the round par-par when — unbeknownst to him — a birdie on either hole would have paired him for the final round with...Fuzzy Zoeller.

Un-Classic Tiger

Buick Classic
Westchester Country Club
Rye, New York
June 19–22

The Tiger Woods-Ernie Els rivalry didn't amount to much at the Buick Classic. Els brought the 'A' game, which enabled him to win the U.S. Open and plenty of confidence. Woods came with a swing that wasn't right, the pressure of public expectation building, and no caddie. Game, set, match to Els.

Els took it right down to the wire, again beating Jeff Maggert to the finish in a rain-interrupted event. The victory moved Els past Woods to the top of the world rankings. Els loves the Buick Classic. In four appearances, he's never been lower than fourth. Els toured Westchester at 268, 16 under par, two shots ahead of Maggert. It was Els' second straight win in the Buick Classic. "This must be my golf course," Els said.

Frankly, Els had braced himself for a letdown. He didn't know how he'd play coming off such a huge victory at Congressional and he was prepared, more or less, for the worst. But he got off to a quick start — a first-round 64, with a 31 on the front — and that allowed him to settle down. "I was worried about focus," Els said. "But my start with two birdies got my mind on golf again."

Woods never really got his mind on golf. There were too many distractions.

Mike "Fluff" Cowan wasn't at Woods' side for the first time since Tiger turned professional. Cowan attended the funeral of Jeff

"Squeeky" Medlen, who had died of leukemia. Medlen was Nick Price's caddie during Price's best years. Cowan was back on the bag for Saturday's third round, but Woods' 72-72 start left him far off the torrid pace set by Els. Woods, who finished 19 shots back, made no excuses about Cowan's absence.

Instead, he talked again about the issue of comprehending and dealing with the magnitude of Tigermania. He was looking for advice, but there was no precedent with which to work.

"Arnold has given me some advice, but he's never dealt with the volume of people that I have to deal with. Plus the generations have changed, too. People are not as courteous as they used to be.... We are definitely not as respectful as we used to be.

"People have a direct effect on how I play. It's a little more difficult. It's a little more with the public. Then again, it gives you the personal touch as well. There are both positives and negatives."

Maggert got an up close and personal look at Woods' galleries. He was Tiger's playing partner the first two rounds at the Buick Classic. Maggert referred to the obnoxious behavior of some galleryites, even those who supported Woods. The whooping and hollering was getting out of control, and nobody knew that better than Woods.

"We need to have it quiet. People want to stand out and make some funny comments. They think it's funny, but to us, we take it a little differently."

The huge galleries not only created sound and movement problems, they were in large part responsible for the funereal pace of play in and around Woods' groups. In the final round of the U.S. Open, the pairing of Woods and Nick Faldo was "put on the clock" by USGA officials. Neither player is known for playing particularly fast — Nick Price ripped Faldo at the British Open for his tortoise-like pace — but they could blame the galleries with some justification. An angry Faldo did so. "We paid for the media," the Englishman said at Congressional. "We lost five minutes (waiting for photographers and film crews to maneuver into place) and they made us speed it up. That's my official comment." Woods and Faldo were timed for six holes, caught up to the pace, and were not penalized. But it was becoming a greater problem each week.

Woods gave another of his junior clinics before the Buick Classic. This one had an unusual backdrop — the skyscrapers of Manhattan and the Harlem River. Woods appeared before some 2,000 youngsters at the Randalls Island Family Golf Center and captivated the audience. He spoke, they listened, and his eloquence was worthy of a much more experienced orator.

"I am going to open my heart to all of you and I hope you take what I have to say and use it.

"No one has the guts, no one takes the time, no one has the patience to stand up and become a role model. Everything is always focused on 'me'. Me, me, me. What can you do for me? It's not about that. It's what can you do for others. Opening up your heart, opening up the love that each one of us is capable of giving."

At his clinics, Woods answers questions and offers tips, and in some cases gives some individual instruction. He talks about the importance of family and education and staying away from drugs. He talks about hard work and dedication and determination.

"The guy upstairs gave me some talent to play this game. People fail to realize I worked my butt off to get where I'm at."

In his absence, Cowan was replaced by a friend, Tim Boardman, for the second round. It marked the first time in his professional career that someone other than Fluff strolled the fairways alongside Woods.

Woods and Cowan, who had caddied for Peter Jacobsen for 19 years before joining Team Tiger, forged quite a relationship in a short time. When Woods turned pro, Jacobsen was sidelined with a back injury. Fluff took Woods' bag on a short-term basis. But Fluff — a self-described child of the '60s and disciple of the late Jerry Garcia and the Grateful Dead — was stunned by what he saw. The scope of Woods' game was breathtaking. When Cowan watched Woods carry a bunker from 264 yards with a 3-wood — carry it easily — he whistled softly. Fluff was soaring, too. He was standing right there next to the phenom and witnessing history in the making. When Woods offered him the job full-time, Cowan jumped at the chance.

"He's been a great friend. He's been a guy to go and talk to about anything at any given time. He's almost like a big brother. Not while we're playing, but off the course. He's been there before. He knows how people handle it. He's been there with Peter. He's definitely passing his experiences on to me, for sure. Mike knows my game. He knows my temperament.

"When I ask him something, he's not afraid to voice his opinion. He's not a 'yes man'. He'll give you an opinion straight out."

Typically, Cowan downplayed his role. "He lets me caddie, he lets me do my job," he said. "Put it that way."

July

Charge of the Woods Brigade

Motorola Western Open
Cog Hill Golf Club
Lemont, Illinois
July 3–6

*T*he scene was a mixed metaphor, as incongruous as the Pied Piper meets the Charge of the Light Brigade. As Tiger Woods strode down the 18th fairway at Cog Hill Golf Club, the adoring gallery — a record crowd of 49,462 turned out for Sunday's final round — scampered through the security barrier. Together, Woods and Tiger's Troops marched up the fairway to victory. It is a scene reminiscent of the British Open, but this was suburban Chicago, not Carnoustie or Royal Lytham or the Old Course at St. Andrews. It certainly wasn't about tradition. Rather, it was about a young golfing superstar who is changing the way Americans view the game and its various codes.

Tiger Woods was about to win again, for the fourth time in 1997, and the gallery wanted to get as close as possible, to feel the moment, to embrace it, to be a part of it.

Tiger Woods didn't look back. He never does. The objective was in front of him several hundred yards and Tiger always looks forward. But the thundering hordes were behind him.

"I definitely heard them."

More importantly, all the other golfers were behind Woods, too. They had pursued but had not caught. There was more than a security rope keeping them short of Woods. There was a chasm, because when Woods is on his game the obstacle is significant. Woods arrived at Cog Hill not knowing exactly where his game stood. He had been struggling. In a dozen previous rounds, he had failed to break par 11 times, and had finished 67th, 19th and 43rd in the last three events. That was after 11 straight rounds under par. Woods didn't try to play his way out of the minislump. Instead, he went home for rest and relaxation. He did a little fishing, a lot of sleeping, and plenty of TV watching.

"Mostly, I was a couch potato."

Woods' playing partners in the first round of the Western Open were Mark O'Meara, his buddy, and John Cook. Few people, and certainly nobody on the PGA Tour, know Woods' game better than O'Meara. On the first hole at Cog Hill's Dubsdread course, Woods laced a 3-wood down the middle of the fairway, hit a sand wedge to within two feet, and made the putt for birdie. Next hole, it was a driver, 3-iron to the front edge, pitch to two feet. Another birdie. O'Meara knew this act. "I'd say he's fine," he said.

All told, Woods needed just 67 strokes — 5 under par — to negotiate Dubsdread, and had issued fair warning.

"I was fresh, ready to go. The last few weeks, I've been kind of tired. When I went home, I just put the clubs away for a little bit. And I felt rejuvenated."

O'Meara issued his own heads-up. "If he keeps playing the way he's playing, he's going to be tough on the weekend," he said. What he already knew, everybody else was about to find out.

"Any time you slump, you just go back to fundamentals. You start from ground one and work your way back up, and that's exactly what I did. I tore my swing apart, worked from the ground back up. Same thing with my putting stroke, and yeah, it's coming around.

"I've never played tournament golf for an entire year. I've played too much too soon sometimes, and I've played not enough. I'm trying to find the right balance. The hard part is trying to keep up your intensity every tournament."

Woods and the Western have a history. He played in the tournament twice as an amateur, making the cut as a 19-year-old in 1995 by shooting 74-71-79-69 for a 293. It was the second cut he had made on the PGA Tour, the first coming in The Masters that year, where he tied for 41st (72-72-77-72 for a 293).

"I've had some pretty good experiences here, some real good positive memories."

A victory in 1997 would do nothing but enhance his fuzzy feelings about the Western Open. He shot a final-round 68 for 275 — 13 under par — and a 3-shot victory over Frank Nobilo. Steve Lowery and Justin Leonard also were in the hunt down the stretch, but Woods' mastery on the par 3s was the determining factor.

Woods birdied three of the short holes, but the 2 at the 14th hole should have told contenders all they needed to know. There was some divine intervention at Cog Hill. Woods' tap-in birdie at the 167-yard 14th — almost an ace — came off a somewhat errant tee shot that floated to the right but caught a fortuitous bounce and rolled next to the cup. Woods almost looked embarrassed by the good fortune.

"The golfing gods were definitely looking down upon me.

"I overcut the shot. It wasn't a very good shot. It almost went into the bunker. I got a good break."

It was more than that, of course. Woods, when he's on, can win in several ways. With skill, with nerve, with desire and, perhaps most telling of all, with his mind.

Nobilo, the bearded stalker from New Zealand, cringed when the birdie 2 was posted. "That was like a knife in the back," he said. "When he's in position to win, he hardly ever goes backward. He seems to birdie the holes he needs to. If he won three or four more, no one would be drastically surprised. Everything is going positive in Tiger's life. I was like a lot of people last year who thought it would take him two years to win one. Like many other people, I was proven wrong."

"If I play my normal game, I should be able to win. The big thing is to have the belief that you can win. Nicklaus had that.

"Look back? It does no good. I have to finish...finishing out the hole is not behind me."

Only the fans are back there, and they're closing in like the Charge of the Light Brigade.

Nay, Laddie

The 126th Open Championship
Royal Troon
Troon, Scotland
July 17–20

The village of Troon, near the Firth of Clyde on Scotland's west coast, has 15,000 residents and five courses, including Royal Troon, one of the majestic layouts which comprise the British Open rota. Troon is home to Colin Montgomerie, Europe's dominant golfer the past five years. Montgomerie's father, James, was the secretary of Royal Troon until his retirement in August 1997. Young Colin learned his golf on the nearby boys' course and, upon coming of age, graduated to Royal Troon. Colin's return to Royal Troon for the first time as a British Open contestant was a headline grabber and had the townsfolk abuzz. But the Scots know golf, and they knew — even the gentle people of Troon, who can tell you stories about Colin Montgomerie's boyhood — that it wasn't possible to discuss the 126th British Open Championship without mentioning the young American, Tiger Woods.

The headlines in the British newspapers — the reputable mainstream media and infamous tabloids alike — preceded Woods' arrival on the British Isles. They were many, they were colorful and, indeed, some were raucous. The risque headlines are normally reserved for celebrities — the Royal Family and superstars in the fields of entertainment, fashion, and sports. Woods fit nicely, which explained the two-page spread which greeted him on the eve of the Open Championship, linking Woods in a love triangle with super model Tyra Banks and Michael Johnson, the Olympic gold medalist. The headline blared, "I'm terrified of losing Tiger!" It called Woods a "smitten kitten...Tiger is crazy about Tyra" and detailed her fears. "She can't decide which one to keep — she's crazy about both of them," said the story, which relied on speculation and innuendo.

Other Tiger headlines included:

"Tiger Almost Blinded in a Mob Frenzy"

"Tiger Maimed by a Ballpoint Pen"

In person, Woods was a charming guest in Scotland. He said and did all the right things, smiled often and pleasantly, and even put his prodigious talent on display occasionally. Great golfers are revered by the Scots. They respect Jack Nicklaus and consider Young Tom Watson, a five-time winner of the Claret Jug, as one of their own. In the right pubs along Portland Street, Troon's cobblestoned main artery, under the right circumstances — if the wind and cold are up and a few pints of beer are required to warm the night — you might even run into a caddie who will swear Young Tom Watson is a distant relative of Old Tom Morris. The affection for Watson runs deep.

The Scots do not yield such respect easily. They respond to only excellent golf, and while they were anxious to get their first look at Woods as a professional, they weren't ready to embrace him. Not yet. That, he had to earn. Woods started the mission by tossing bouquets to the golf fans of Great Britain.

"This is the home of golf. This is probably the biggest tournament to win in the world, just because it is definitely the world open. You get the best players here, the traditions, and you play on a traditional golf course. I love to play links courses. That's what it's all about.

"I have noticed people here are very respectful. When we say now is not the time for autographs or anything like that, please wait until later, they don't complain about it. They accept it. That's been awfully nice. Also, they don't cheer for shots that just get airborne here. People here understand you are not here just to sign autographs and take pictures. You are here to play a golf tournament. They understand that."

Woods played in two British Opens as an amateur. He finished joint 68th in 1995 on the Old Course at St. Andrews and joint 22nd in 1996 at Royal Lytham, where he finished with rounds of 66-70-70 after an opening 75. He had a rousing conclusion to Royal Lytham — 6 birdies on the final 11 holes. The memory of that finish and the resurgence of his game — with the victory at the Western Open — bolstered Woods' confidence. His standard pre-tournament "I expect to win every tournament" line was greeted by raised eyebrows in Europe. Woods explained.

"That's my goal...my philosophy. I'm not going to change. I do not come here just to play golf. I come here to do the best I can. That's to try and win. That's a goal I have. I don't want to step on any toes, but if you ask me a question I'm going to answer the question very honestly, and that's my goal going into every tournament."

The British bookies established Woods as the 5-to-1 favorite, the lowest odds ever, and braced themselves. A $10 million payout was expected in the event Woods won, a result Steve Elkington didn't think was far-fetched. "When he wins he always comes back and wins again," said Elkington, Woods' playing partner for the first two rounds at Royal Troon. "He's not one of those guys who drops off after he wins. He hits the ball so far that a lot of these (fairway) bunkers...I mean this course is very old. He wouldn't even notice if there was a guy lying in there dead as he walked by. I mean, are you kidding? He can probably hit a 3-iron over those bunkers."

Woods and his swing guru, Butch Harmon, worked on swing plane.

"I'm swinging a lot better now. I still need to do some work and see the golf course a couple more times. Royal Troon is definitely different than my other two British Open experiences because the other two courses I was able to see the course in front of me. Here there are a couple of blind tee shots. It's definitely a golf course on which you have to know your lines and trust them.

"I tried to get my [swing] plane a little better. It's been off. My ball flight has been fluctuating. I'm trying to work on my plane and some other little positions here and there. When that happens, my

ball flight comes down naturally. Those are things I tried to work on at home and I have touched up on this week with Butch."

Two other issues — death threats and race — dominated the debriefing, with the British tabloids turning each into banner headlines.

On death threats:

"I receive numerous death threats and hate mail. That's nothing unusual. I remember in Phoenix — definitely one of the rowdier crowds on our Tour — I came off the green and security completely broke down. They just absolutely mobbed me and knocked me down. I was trying to sign autographs as I was going along. Unfortunately, people have pens and one of them cut me under the eye. It can get hairy at times, but on our Tour that has been rectified. Security is much better and people are learning."

On race:

"When you are playing in a sport in which you are not the majority — you're the minority — of course there is going to be some animosity. That's the way it goes. It was like that for Arthur Ashe and Jackie Robinson and numerous other professional athletes. Until we understand and respect everyone for the kind of person they are, not just by looking at pigmentation, that's going to be there."

♉︎♑︎

Tiger Woods' pigmentation after the first round was blue. He shot 1-over-par 72, with a triple-bogey 7 on the difficult 11th hole, Railway. His tee shot on the 463-yard par 4 found the thornbushes. He took an unplayable lie and dropped in the rough. From there, he boldly tried to play out with a 2-iron — a youthful mistake — and it cost him again. The ball caught the hill in front of him and dropped down, leaving him 120 yards to the hole. His 8-iron into the wind sailed over the green. He chipped back to six feet and two-putted.

A brisk north wind, the prevailing direction, with gusts to 30 miles an hour, turned the back nine into a battlefield, quite appropriate for a course that has a hole, the seventh — Tel-el-Kebir — commemorating an 1882 battle in the Sudan. Players got under par on the front and backpedaled on the back. The gusty winds sweeping across Royal Troon put a loop in a lot of golf swings. For once, everybody else's swing looked like Jim Furyk's action, and that gave Furyk, an emerging star on the PGA Tour, a decided advantage. He shot 67 — 4 under par — to tie Darren Clarke of Northern Ireland for the lead.

Woods' round included a 435-yard drive, downwind, at the fourth hole. On the 557-yard par 5, he had a 9-iron left to the green. He two-putted for birdie. Woods, upon questioning, said he once drove a ball 500 yards.

"In Denver, at altitude, so it doesn't really matter. That doesn't count."

Woods was hoping for more of the same kind of weather — brisk and windy.

"What happens when the wind is up like this, if you go out and play a good, solid round and shoot something in the 60s, you're going to pick up a lot of ground and a lot of shots on the field. That's nice — that's very comforting to know, going out. If it doesn't blow and you shoot 67, you just try to keep pace with everybody."

There was no 67 for Tiger in Round II. He slogged it around in 74, 3 over, for 146. At 4 over, he was 13 shots off the pace set by Northern Ireland's Clarke.

For the second straight round, there was a crash after the turn. Woods made a snowman — 8 — on the 10th hole. Again, he got entangled in a gorse bush and whiffed a shot.

" My club went right underneath the ball.
"If you take away those two bad holes, I'm 3 under. I'm not playing that bad. I just happen to have had two bad holes at the wrong time. Hopefully, I'll get off to a good start tomorrow. If I can, the ideal start, which has some easy holes early, [would be to] make some birdies. I'm hitting the ball very well this week."

Woods wasn't throwing in the towel.

"I was more than 13 shots back at Pebble Beach and almost won. I think the golf course is great, a little more severe than the last two I played just because of the undulations in the fairways. That's been a little tricky. You can get some uphill lies going into this wind and you've got to hit some pretty weird clubs."

Like weird science, Woods needed some weird golf over the final 36 holes to raise the Claret Jug.

The weather was perfect yet again Saturday and the education of Tiger Woods continued. He attacked Royal Troon like it has seldom, if ever, been attacked before. He hit only five fairways, but more than made up for it with a brilliant 24-putt effort on greens perfectly suited for him. The putting surfaces at Royal Troon are relatively flat and not especially fast. There was no fear of rolling a putt well past and leaving a knee-knocker. Woods went for everything. He shot a course record–tying 64 for a 210 total after 54 holes. That's 3 under par, and it left him 8 shots behind the leader, Sweden's Jesper Parnevik.

In typical Woods fashion, he zoomed from a tie for 49th to a tie for eighth and set his jaw for the final round.

"Honestly, I think I still can [win]. Whether it happens or not, we'll see."

Parnevik rolled his eyes at the suggestion, and said, "I am sure he can shoot close to zero on this course if he gets everything going.... We know he can shoot 59 any time he wants."

Woods' 64 matched Greg Norman's number in the final round of the 1989 championship at Royal Troon. On that occasion, Norman erased a 7-shot deficit but lost to American Mark Calcavecchia in a four-hole playoff. When Norman shot 64, the par was 72. With the 11th hole — Railway — shortened by 18 yards, to 463 yards, the par in 1997 was 71. Woods made seven birdies, an eagle, and two bogeys. With justification, those two bogeys had Woods mulling the possibility of going even lower. On Saturday, moving day, he had to go low, and he did.

"I had to do it. It's nice when everything works out just the way you want it. Put it this way: my last two days I've hit the ball very well and haven't got a lot out of my rounds, and today I said, 'Just hit the ball the way you have been and make some putts. Eliminate that one high score and you'll be all right.'

"That's exactly what happened."

Woods escaped the big numbers that plagued him in the first two rounds. He made a triple-bogey 7 on the 11th hole in the opening round and shot 72. In the second round, he made a triple-bogey 8 on the 10th hole while shooting 74. Woods was 2 shots better at the 11th for a bogey 5, but he called it the key to his round — more important even than an eagle at 16. After hitting a 3-wood off the tee and into a gorse bush, he extricated himself with three sand wedge shots, the last of which left him four feet from the cup. He nailed the bogey putt.

"Making bogeys like that are what saves rounds. If I'd have made double there, losing two shots, you feel like throwing some stuff away. Getting up and down from 71 yards definitely makes you feel pretty good about yourself. Then I took a chance on the next hole, which I haven't done all week, to see if I could squeeze out a birdie, and that's exactly what happened."

Among those congratulating Woods on the remarkable achievement was the Duke of York, Prince Andrew. It was Andrew's estranged wife, Sarah Ferguson, who had greeted Woods behind the 18th green with a hug following his victory at the Byron Nelson Classic in May.

Woods couldn't squeeze blood out of a turnip, nor par out of the Postage Stamp, and that was his undoing in the final round.

The Postage Stamp is one of the most famous holes in all of golfdom. It is a mere 126 yards, a flip wedge for the great modern ballstrikers, but its history and glory are unmatched. The No. 8 hole got its name from the size of the green — it is the size of a postage stamp. The green is surrounded by bunkers and sits beneath a mound to the left. A ball moving left to right can hit the mound or even the left side of the green and spin entirely off into the bunkers on the right. Anything long is lost in gorse. Anything short, ditto.

A German amateur, Herman Tissies, made a 15 there in 1950. Twenty-three years later, Gene Sarazen, then 71, licked the Postage Stamp twice. He played it twice and never used his putter. In the first round, Sarazen aced the hole with a 5-iron. The next day, Sarazen holed a bunker shot for 2.

When Woods was asked his impression of No. 8 on the eve of the tournament, he couldn't remember the hole and, much to the dismay of the assembled media from the United Kingdom, had to be prompted. A few days later, that moment would drip with irony.

Finally, Woods said,

"The short par 3. OK, yeah. Definitely a short hole."

But great holes don't have to be long. It was the shortest hole at Royal Troon that capsized Woods.

When dawn broke Sunday along the Firth of Clyde, the western horizon was glistening and, for the third straight day, there was barely a touch of breeze. It unsettled the Scots, who abide by the saying, "Nay wind, nay rain, nay golf." The townsfolks of Troon didn't want frightful conditions, for fear it would lead to a fluke champion. Colin Cotter is a caddie at Royal Troon, one of the finest at the old links. He knows every fertile inch, from the sea to the wee eighth to the impossible Railway and the burn that crosses the 16th fairway. Cotter, expressing the sentiments of the residents, wanted an honest breeze, the prevailing wind out of the northwest, because he wanted Royal Troon to be Royal Troon, to be at its best so that the champion golfer, whoever that might be, would be a worthy champion. The sentiments were sincere but, in truth, Troon resembled San Diego or Augusta, Georgia, not the fearsome Scottish links it truly is. There's more wind in Texas than there was on the Ayrshire coast of Scotland in the third week of July.

Woods' last hurrah at Royal Troon began with a mighty par save at the first hole, where he drove into the right rough. His trusty sand wedge got tangled in the tall grasses, the shaft turned over, and he yanked his second shot into the front left bunker. He got it up and down and strode briskly to the second tee. He figured to need at least two birdies on the first three holes if there was to be a heroic rally, but he parred the first three instead. He reached the par 5 4th hole in two shots and two-putted for birdie, then made an unexpected birdie at the long par 3 5th hole to bolster his spirits. Now, another par 5 — the sixth — awaited, and in the next stretch of three holes he could still get into the middle of things. He was 2 under par for the round — and 5 under par for the championship — as he stood on the tee of the 577-yard 6th. That's as close as he would get to glory at Troon.

Woods missed a short birdie putt at No. 6. At the 7th, he took dead aim and scorched a driver that wound up in the front right green guarding the 402-yard par 4. His long explosion may have been one of his best shots of the tournament, finishing just a few feet from another possible birdie. But Woods missed again. His first putt from three feet never hit the hole and Woods glared at his Titleist putter.

"If I had made those two putts, I might have got going. It would have gotten me to 7-under."

At least he had not dropped any shots through seven holes. That changed at the Postage Stamp.

Woods selected a 9-iron for the tee shot — the same club he had used for his hole-in-one earlier in the year in Phoenix — and hit it into a bunker on the right. His first attempt to extricate the ball failed and it rolled back in. Indifferently, he chopped the next out some 25 to 30 feet left of the pin — not the place to be — and completed the debacle with three putts.

"I knew I couldn't win after that. I was too far back."

Woods, who was tied for fifth place standing on the 6th tee, dropped into a tie for 24th with a final round 74.

The champion golfer for 1997 was, indeed, a young American, Justin Leonard, 25, who learned his game in Texas, where the wind blows and dust covers the air like a tumbleweed blanket. Leonard's gutsy victory, from 5 shots behind Parnevik at the start of the final round, signaled a call to arms and a changing of golf's guard. That was the unmistakable conclusion at Royal Troon. Tiger Woods, 21, had won The Masters, and Ernie Els, 27, the "Big Cat" from South Africa, captured the U.S. Open. Now, another twenty-something was reigning supreme in Scotland — the home of golf.

"Being five back, I had maybe a little more relaxed attitude," said Leonard, the youngest British Open winner since 1979, when Seve Ballesteros won it at 22. "Maybe having seen Tiger do so well, having seen Ernie do so well, maybe I thought it's OK to go out and win a tournament like this being the age I am. Maybe that was in the back of my mind somewhere."

Golf, long maligned for having no superstars on its horizons, was unveiling its young lions on the world stage. But something was missing. Leonard, like Tiger and the Big Cat, needed a nickname to complement the theme. Easy enough. Leonard the Lionheart.

August

Tigermania Hits Motown

Buick Open
Warwick Hills Golf & Country Club
Grand Blanc, Michigan
August 7–10

Grand Blanc is a small town 60 miles north of Detroit, just south of Flint on Interstate 75, which bisects Michigan from the Ohio border to the Mackinac Bridge, the only physical link between the Lower and Upper peninsulas of the Great Lakes State. Flint is the world headquarters for the Buick Motor Division of General Motors, the largest automaker on the planet. Buick owns another distinction, this relating to professional golf.

In 1958, Buick became the first corporate sponsor of a PGA Tour event when the Buick Open was played at Warwick Hills Golf and Country Club in Grand Blanc. In 1997, it was the oldest corporate sponsor on the Tour. Its relationship has grown to include four Tour events, placed strategically and geographically around the United States for maximum visibility. Buick also has been the official car of the PGA Tour since 1984. The wisdom of Buick's decision years ago to become involved with professional golf is undeniable. There isn't a major automaker worldwide that isn't affiliated, in one form or another, with golf these days. The obvious reason is that the demographics work.

In the early 1990s, with Buick's clout with the Tour growing, the Buick Open was moved into a slot just before the PGA Championship. It dramatically improved the caliber of the fields — the Buick Open became a final chance for a pre-major tune-up — and the biggest names in the game began showing up. Greg Norman. Nick Faldo. Nick Price. Fred Couples. Add another factor to the equation — the emergence of the Ryder Cup Matches every two years as a major international sporting event. Every other year, that gives golfers another reason to visit Grand Blanc.

The captain of the United States Ryder Cup team — in 1997 it was Tom Kite — adds two wild card selections to the 10 golfers who automatically qualify by accruing points over a two-year period. The captain's choices are announced on the Monday after the PGA Championship. The Buick Open, therefore, is the second to last chance to gain points. Failing that, it becomes the second to last chance to impress the captain sufficiently to be considered for a wild card berth. In 1995, Couples played well enough at the Buick Open to convince then captain Lanny Wadkins that his ailing back could withstand the rigors of playing up to five rounds of golf over three days in the Ryder Cup format. Wadkins picked Couples.

The Buick Open had one other thing going for it in 1997 — Tiger Woods.

Woods prepared for the first three majors of the year by taking the previous week off to hone his game in private, study under his swing tutor Butch Harmon, and brace himself for the crush that awaits him at the four biggest events on the golf calendar. Based on that, Buick officials weren't building up their hopes, for fear of disappointment. The spirits of tournament officials were buoyed three weeks before when *The Detroit News* reported from the British Open in Troon, Scotland, that Woods would indeed be coming to Grand Blanc. The officials remained cautiously optimistic, but could offer nothing definite on Woods' plans. If they knew and were playing dumb, they did a good job.

They had a predicament. They wanted to be able to tell everybody Woods was coming — ticket sales and anticipation for their event would soar wildly. But they had to be careful. They didn't want to promote something that might not happen. The fallout from unkept promises would be damaging. So whenever there were calls to the tournament office — and there were plenty — asking for confirmation of the newspaper stories that Woods was coming, Buick Open officials were noncommittal, but in a positive way. They answered inquiries by saying that *The Detroit News* and the writer had credibility and could be believed if that's what was being reported.

A week before the tournament, Tiger frenzy already was hitting hard. Phones were ringing off the hook with questions about ticket availability and other matters pertinent to spectators. At mid-afternoon on the Friday before the Buick Open, several hours before the player commitment deadline, Tournament Director J. Schaffer got the phone call he was waiting for.

"Tiger is coming," Schaffer said.

Roll the presses. Print more tickets.

"It feels really good," Schaffer said. "There's just been an exciting feel around here and this rounds it out. It's the first time (in 39 years) that we've had the Masters, the U.S. Open and the British Open champions here and we couldn't be happier. It's been hectic...it'll build up about 10 notches now."

Justin Leonard, the British Open champion, was the defending champion at the Buick Open. Els, the U.S. Open champion, had played well at Warwick Hills on his earlier visit and contemplated a successful tournament. Els also had won the Buick Classic, making him sort of an ex-officio winner at the Buick Open and a darling of the Buick crowd.

The estimates of what the crowd might be were doubled, up to 200,000 for the week, and Schaffer needed more tickets. "We've never had a second printing yet," he said. "That's something we're going to have to consider now. We've never run out before. I think we're pretty close to being out of daily tickets. I know we're getting pretty low in our supply based on what we usually print. It doesn't mean we can't print more."

Detroit and its environs braced for the attack of Tigermania.

Michigan is a golfing hotbed. It has more public courses than any state in the union — a little known fact nationally — and it's among the United States' most prominent centers for minority golf. The person most responsible for that is Selina "Hollywood" Johnson, an African-American who is the patron saint of inner-city golf. Johnson has known Tiger and his family for years through her involvement with junior golf. Like Buick Open officials, she hoped for the best without letting herself get too optimistic. When Tiger announced he would come to Detroit, there was no masking Johnson's joy. There would be no clinic this time — something Johnson was secretly hoping for — but she knew that before long Woods would have a clinic for Detroit and Johnson's kids.

"I'm ecstatic," Selina Johnson said. "My kids are going to be there to watch him, to idolize him, to do all of that — it's just exciting. Since he has established a pattern of not making all of the tournaments, I'm delighted he has decided to come here. Tiger has put a spark in the eyes of all children regardless of a family's financial background, regardless of geographics."

Johnson should know. Participation in her program has soared. By mid-1997, she had up to 1,200 inner-city youngsters in various recreational and school programs.

"Two years ago you couldn't have gotten kids from the inner city to migrate to golf," she said. "Many young people who never thought of golf as an avenue to attend college now have that opportunity. Kids see a young man making the playing field level and they are inspired. Inner-city kids know it is possible, it is a reality. Their attitude is, 'He has done it and we can, too.' I'm just thrilled when I see kids who never wanted to play golf coming into the game and speaking about golf in a different way."

It was a glorious week in Grand Blanc. The crowds were enormous, enthusiastic, and well-behaved.

Woods' decision to play at Warwick Hills was based on several factors. Prominent among them was the golf course itself, and the recommendation of "Fluff" Cowan. Cowan had been coming to the Buick Open for years. He knew the course to be a classic design with tree-lined fairways that was always in great shape. Cowan also knew Woods would have some serious fun at Warwick Hills, a 7,105-yard layout that played right into the strength of golf's longest hitter. It's not a course that takes the driver out of play, and Woods wanted to focus on his driving game heading into the PGA Championship at Winged Foot Golf Club, a grand old course with ancient trees that smother the fairways. The tournament record at the Buick Open is 26 under par, by Robert Wrenn, and Cowan suspected his man could go very low. The notion appealed to Woods, especially the part where he could work on the driver.

Cowan, whose knowledge of the course was instrumental in Woods' success at Augusta National, also knows Warwick Hills. He was on the bag when Peter Jacobsen won the Buick Open in 1980. "It was the first victory for both of us," Cowan said. "It was special. I remember he was six, seven shots back going into the final round and went out and played a very solid round of golf. I want to say it was 65 or 66 [it was 67]." That bit of trivia would be important a few days later.

Cowan, his fame soaring, was mobbed by the media after Woods' Tuesday practice round. He handled it with typical aplomb. Standing under a tree near the first tee at Warwick Hills, he talked at some length about his expectations upon joining Team Tiger. "I didn't have any expectations. Expectations are not a healthy thing. That's why I try not to have any," he said. He talked about the financial windfall caddying for Woods. "Money isn't comfort. Comfort is love, a good bed, caring friends, and a happy dog," he said.

The commercial endorsements continued to come Cowan's way, however, and he had six offers to do a book about his life with Tiger. But Cowan has been around. He knows the ropes. He knows Woods is the man and Fluff would never do anything to overshadow him. That's not how it works.

"At times, I'm amazed [by Tigermania]," Cowan said. "He is a great player, but he's just another human being. It's amazing how people gravitate toward him."

Woods gave the local media some terrific sound bites at his press debriefing. By his standards, it was a small, cozy gathering, but Woods went through the entire range of questions and answers, and never made it seem like it was an imposition. It was easy to see that his comfort level was rising.

"This is a part of what I have to do to play my sport. If this is what I have to deal with, then that's fine, because I love to play.

"What you have to remember is [the fans] come out to support you. They're not out there to boo you — there are no hometown favorites in golf."

He was particularly effusive when the topic switched to the Ryder Cup and the success of Generation X.

"I play an individual sport where I'm out there by myself. When you play for your team, for your country, the pride swells up. I'll never forget the World Cup in France my freshman year in college. When our flag was raised, the tears were flowing down my face — and everybody else's on the team. That's when you know you're playing for more than just yourself. You're playing for your teammates, for your captain, for your parents, for your country."

Woods proved it wasn't just lip service. On Saturday, after the third round of the Buick Open, he returned to his hotel room and placed a long distance call to Scarsdale, New York, and Quaker Ridge Golf Club, site of the Walker Cup, the amateur version of the Ryder Cup. The American Walker Cup team, of which Woods was a member in 1995, had a commanding lead in the competition and was certain to regain the trophy. The American team was out to dinner, so Woods left his hotel phone and room numbers. When Captain Downing Gray returned the call, Woods spoke to each of the American golfers, offering encouragement. Ironically, the United States had lost two years earlier with the great amateur Tiger Woods on the team. If he didn't play the Buick Open, Woods had told Gray, he would be at Quaker Ridge in support.

"I played for Downing and he's the best. A lot of the guys on the team are my good friends, either through college or through amateur golf, or through the previous Walker Cup. I felt that since I couldn't be there that I wanted to tell them I'm there in spirit and supporting them and told all of them to bring that cup back to the United States."

The Americans won handily, 18-6.

The winning ways of the PGA Tour's Young Lions was also a focal point during the Buick Open. Leonard was the defending champion, and Els — until a final-round collapse — looked like he would win in a walk.

"It's not necessarily a new breed — it's our generation. It's a generation that is a lot more flamboyant. Definitely a more aggressive generation, not afraid to take risks. I've seen Phil Mickelson try to go over water to a green with a fairway wood. [The older golfers] play the percentages. Sometimes we don't make the right play, but Generation X as a whole is a lot more aggressive."

Woods also said things like Tom Watson and Tom Kite — great though they were — had seen their best days and were on the way out. Typically, the media was quick to deliver Woods' message to the older players and solicit a response. The debate was a source of amusement to Greg Norman. "I remember when everyone was saying just recently that no one but international players were winning majors," the Shark said. "Then it was said that no Americans had won, then no internationals were winning, so it's whatever you guys [the media] want to pick up and run with.

"It's just the way of things and that doesn't mean to say that they're going to win every major from here on in. I can remember when guys in their 40s won majors one year. The Nicklauses, the Floyds, the Irwins, so just don't read into it because there are a lot of other golfers out there. We all relish and cherish the fact that young fellows do come along at a young age with the mind-set that they can go out there and blitz them, and win, and we've seen that happen for years. But it's how they continue on that it's all about."

A week later, at the PGA Championship at Winged Foot Golf Club, the great man himself, Jack Nicklaus, was asked to comment. No, he said, the old guard isn't through. "All guards change," Nicklaus said. "I don't think there's any question about that. I'm still hanging around here and my guard's changed two or three times since I've really competed. I love to play, I love to be around and I'm sure that Watson and Kite will be around." On one point, Nicklaus didn't disagree. "The game is for young players right now," he said. "It's a game for powerful players, but experience still counts for a lot when you come to the major championships. It always has. I don't see those (older) guys disappearing overnight."

Kite also referred at the PGA Championship to Woods' commentary. "I read in the paper the other day that Tiger thought that Tom [Watson] and I were fairly good players at one time," Kite said. "So since I was a fairly good player at one time I thought I'd better show up."

Woods teed it up at 7 A.M. Tuesday for a practice round at Warwick Hills to avoid the crowds. No luck.

"It's unreal when you have a thousand people out there following you in the morning. I'd be asleep."

On the 17th tee, Woods and Cowan had a short exchange. Then Cowan — once a fine college player and still a low-handicap golfer — grabbed a club out of the bag and hit a shot at the 197-yard par 3. The ball finished short of the green and to the right. Asked about the shot later, Cowan denied ever attempting it and deadpanned: "I don't know what you think you saw." The gallery loved the interaction and Woods was impressed.

"It was his first swing in a couple of weeks. I thought it was pretty good."

The gallery was no less attentive the next day during the pro-am. Woods' group of amateurs included Nick Saban, the popular Michigan State University football coach. Saban was duly impressed by Woods' athleticism and dedication. "He's proud of the fact that he lifts weights a few times a week," Saban said. "He's a good athlete. He's proud of his father, who was a catcher with the Kansas City Monarchs. Tiger pitched a little as a kid and said one of his favorite memories is pitching to his dad."

Saban, like all football coaches, sized Woods up in football terms. "A wide receiver or a cornerback," he said.

Woods shot 74 and the pro-am team posted a 15-under-par 57.

"We never talked football, never talked golf...we talked about life, balance, things we believe in."

Woods wasn't on top of his game in the opening round at Warwick Hills, something he blamed on his inactivity. He had been idle since the British Open and said that when he broke his golf bag out of cold storage before the Buick, moths flew out. He brought it back in Round II with a 4-under-par 68, but with Els starting 67-64 to get to 13-under, Tiger found himself 9 shots back.

"I hit it better. I was more intense. I managed my game a little better. You can't make it all back in one day. You've got to keep shooting under par. I have to start playing better, give myself chances."

It didn't happen in the third round. Woods made an annoying double bogey at the easy 10th hole, a 401-yard par 4 that's usually no more than driver-wedge. It neutralized an eagle at the first hole and had Woods angry with himself.

"Dumb mental mistakes."

Els had a chance to run away from the field and hide. He couldn't do it. He shot even-par 72 in Saturday's third round and, in his words, let a lot of golfers back into the tournament, Woods among them. Another in the hunt was veteran Curtis Strange, who had not won since the 1989 U.S. Open. "The ball is going where I'm looking most of the time," Strange said. "It's nice. Every Sunday is a shootout on the PGA Tour. It's nice to be a part of one."

On the surface, there wasn't much of a shoot-out in the offing. Els is too good, too confident, too hot. "You don't ever want to be behind Ernie," Strange said.

"Fluff" Cowan shared a little story with Woods about Jacobsen's victory in 1980.

"'Fluff' told me when Jacobsen won he was six back going into the final round."

Woods shot a third-round 70 to reach 6 under, still 7 shots behind Els, but the weather was perfect again for the final round at Warwick Hills and everybody knew Tiger was capable of going very low under the conditions. Cowan had provided the historical perspective and motivation with the Jacobsen anecdote.

Woods went off some 90 minutes before the leaders, Els and Strange in the final group. He had talked about the importance of a hot start to apply some pressure. Once that is accomplished, Warwick Hills becomes a cream puff — the back nine is where birdies can be made in bunches. The 12th and 14th holes are short par 4s, driveable for somebody with Woods' prodigious power. Woods' game plan was to go for the 335-yard 12th and 322-yard 14th if he was hitting it well. There's also a very short par 5, the 13th, and a long but reachable 3-shot hole, the 16th. On Sunday, he had no choice. It was go-for-broke time.

Woods almost hit his first tee shot out of bounds, but recovered and had a 6-foot birdie putt on the first green. He missed. He made bogey at the 4th and the fast start he was looking for had not materialized. He finally made birdie at the 7th hole, a par 5, to go out in 36 strokes.

"I never really got anything going on the front. It was frustrating. I wasn't hitting the ball good enough to get anything going."

Just as promised, he started his move with a birdie at the 12th and made another at the 13th, where he hit a monster 340-yard drive, then reached the green in two but left a 20-foot putt for eagle two inches short. An Arnie-like charge was in the making, and the huge galleries noticed. They flocked to Woods and encircled, several deep, every hole he played — from tee to green — on the back nine. Woods squandered a chance at the 14th, but birdied the 15th and 16th to reach 10 under par. Meanwhile, Els wasn't making any birdies and had come back even more to the field. Now at 12-under, Els was feeling the heat from Vijay Singh. Woods was there, too, but was running out of holes.

"It kind of kicked in. I hit a lot of good shots on the back. You start getting a little confidence in yourself and feel like you can hit shots again."

Singh produced a six-birdie, bogey-free final round to shoot 66 and cruised past Els for the victory. Woods' 68 was good, but not good enough. He finished at 272, 10 under par, 5 shots behind Singh.

Woods, who had changed putters for the final round, was positive about the upcoming PGA Championship.

"I didn't make anything for the first three days. I put it [the putter] in some darkness...punished it big-time."

The Buick Open was noteworthy for something else. Woods' prize money for finishing in a tie for eighth was $43,500. It gave him a total of $1,821,895 — the most ever on the PGA Tour — surpassing the mark established in 1996 by Tom Lehman.

The Passionate Pursuit

PGA Championship
Winged Foot Golf Club
Mamaroneck, New York
August 14–17

The 79th PGA Championship at Winged Foot Golf Club had more angles than Euclidean geometry.

There was the Ryder Cup and the speculation of which two players Tom Kite, captain of the United States team, would pick as his wild cards for the September matches in Spain. The discussions, debates, and media inquiries — to Kite and other players — became so intense that early in the week Davis Love III said the PGA Championship isn't Qualifying School for the Ryder Cup. His comment was on point, but it didn't stop the deliberations.

After all, even Love arrived at Winged Foot with the Ryder Cup on his mind. A week before, at Warwick Hills, Kite had told Love he was on the team, whether he finished in the top 10 or not. Fred Couples, Love's good friend and partner during major international competitions, said he could tell Kite's message had taken a load off DL3. Couples and Love won four straight World Cups for the United States through 1995 and have been paired in the Ryder Cup. Love arrived in Warwick Hills, and again at Winged Foot, holding down the No. 10 spot on the American points list, the final automatic berth. He was in jeopardy of being passed, but now he knew it wouldn't matter.

"I just hadn't been playing that well," Love said. "I didn't want to leave any doubt in anybody's mind on the Ryder Cup or Tom's selections. I didn't want to put any pressure on Tom to have to pick me. If I do have to be picked, I want to go down with a good one and not make him have to think too hard."

The Ryder Cup theme was prevalent as well among the European players and media. The Euros had controversy and speculation of their own, with three marquee players — Nick Faldo, Jose Maria Olazabal, and Jesper Parnevik — in contention for two wild card spots and the possibility that somebody the stature of a Faldo, the kingpin of the European side for two decades, might not make the team. It was fodder for the hot stove but, in reality, there was no chance either Faldo or Olazabal could be omitted, not with the competition slated for Joe Mary's home ground of Spain. Both Parnevik or Faldo desperately wanted the invitation and, as it turned out, would get it. "Would I pick myself?" Parnevik asked. "Yes," came his unabashed answer.

Faldo had appeared on 10 straight Ryder Cup teams, a streak in which the Englishman took great pride: "I wouldn't like to miss out on this at all." What Faldo said and what he did, however, were two different things. The level of Faldo's game didn't match his desire. For him, 1997 was an indifferent year. He won in Los Angeles, at the Nissan Open at Riviera Country Club, but wasn't a threat in any of the majors. Faldo saw the Ryder Cup as a final chance to redeem himself and rescue the year. It was the same scenario as in 1995 when his clutch victory over Curtis Strange in singles matches at Oak Hill was critical to the Europeans' upset triumph. Faldo was willing to take that victory as a comforting thought for the winter months.

This time, Faldo was prepared for the worst. He wouldn't let himself feel slighted if Ballesteros didn't choose in his favor. "Not at all," Faldo said. "Why worry about it? Seve's probably got everything under control, so no problem. But, amazingly, it's talked about more than Tiger.

"Can it be bigger than Tiger? Yeesh."

Leave it to the Europeans to put things into perspective.

For Colin Montgomerie, No. 1 on the European side, the choice was clear-cut.

"A team without Nick Faldo is a worse team," Montgomerie said. "It has to be. Very few people can be 1-up on the first tee, in golf terms, and he's one of those people. We need him. We do. Nobody works at it harder."

Faldo's eventual inclusion onto the team as a wild card set up the possibility of a singles showdown: Faldo vs. Woods. The Terminator vs. The Exterminator.

Angle: The growth of Tiger Woods.

The mainstream golf media is generally divided into two parts. There is a group that covers most of the tournaments, including all the majors, and another group that covers the three American majors and events in their locality. Since many of those writers were not in Scotland for the British Open, it had been nearly two months, since the U.S. Open at Congressional, that they had encountered Tiger.

What they saw was a poised, polished, and much more mature Tiger Woods. During the initial press conference and others featuring Woods during the week, they turned to other reporters who had seen more of Woods in the intervening days and weeks to ask: "How long has he been this good?"

The answer was that the young man had been getting better all along, handling questions with savvy and self-assurance, smiling easily and showing none of the stage fright or reluctance that had marked these sessions months before. He was articulate, but more than that, his words had substance. He answered questions he would not have attempted earlier, when he deflected some inquiries with, 'That's private' or 'That's personal.' When asked about whether Kite had solicited his opinions on the Ryder Cup and the wild card choices, Woods didn't hesitate.

"Jokingly, I said, 'Why don't you put Arnold and Jack on there.' But, honestly, I told him that I felt...politically the best thing to do is pick No. 11 and 12 (on the points list) because they've earned their spots. They've worked hard for two years to get their spots. But you also have to look at who's playing hot, too. If someone is 11 or 12 and playing bad the last few months, then it's questionable. If I was a captain, I would pick guys who were hot right now, who had been playing well and who are in the top 15."

Another angle: Suddenly, there was also a race for Player of the Year honors. Tiger Woods appeared to have it wrapped up through the first six months, but he began to falter while others — Ernie Els, Justin Leonard, and even Phil Mickelson — got back into the fray. The PGA Championship loomed as the tie-breaker.

It is conventional wisdom that two majors beats one major and the money title, which Woods had locked. With two months left in the season, he already was flirting with the $2 million mark. With a second major, Els or Leonard had a chance to steal the honor from Woods and a victory for Mickelson at Winged Foot, coupled with one other — say, the season-ending Tour Championship — would put Lefty in the mix. Woods said so himself the week before at the Buick Open.

"One of us wins the PGA, they should get Player of the Year and they probably will."

Of course, there was also the subject of the twenty-somethings. Every player was asked about it, and it was amplified with the PGA Championship's traditional pairing for the first two rounds. The final major puts the winners of the first three majors together for Friday and Saturday. That means Woods, Els, and Leonard marching down the fairways of Winged Foot side by side for 36 holes. It was wonderful stuff. The galleries loved it, the media devoured it, and the golfers reveled in it.

"It's fun playing with the youngsters," said Els, the graybeard at 27.

"We were all pretty relaxed — we had a few laughs out there," said Leonard, 25.

"You could definitely feel the positive energy."

Leonard played a great opening round, shooting 68 — 2 shots better than Woods and Els — but the British Open champion was grim-faced. There was so much congestion around the group that the flow was disrupted. Movement from green to tee resembled rush hour in Times Square. It was gridlock. The entourage inside the ropes included police, marshals, officials, security, media, and photographers.

But among the strengths of Leonard's game is, as Tom Kite said in Scotland, "setting his jaw" and excelling under the most challenging circumstances. Leonard was in his element. He saved the round with some uncanny saves on the back nine, requiring a mere 12 putts over the final 10 holes. He had six one-putts — one for birdie, the others to save par. Woods was enthralled.

"Justin was making some unbelievable pars."

The performance resembled Leonard's magic on the back nine of the opening round at Royal Troon, where he hit no greens in regulation yet shot even par. "I was looking forward to playing with Tiger and Ernie," Leonard said. "But it was a shock to see that many people inside the ropes. I played with Tiger last week (at the Buick Open) and it was a very different scene. It's the last major of the year so I guess there's a few more people here."

Woods got to 3 under par before a double bogey at the 12th hole — a par 5 of 540 yards — set the tone for his week. He faced an in-between distance and attempted to fade his second shot.

"I only had 240 yards to the front edge. That's not very far for my 3-wood. It was either a nuke 2-iron or a little soft 3-wood."

Woods lofted the 3-wood high and right. It finished under a tree, and when he was done hacking the ball out of Winged Foot's wicked rough, he had made 7.

"You can't afford to hit shots that far off line...and in a major you should be penalized like I have been."

The first-round lead was shared by John Daly and Davis Love III, two long-hitting Americans who shot 4-under-par 66 to tie the course record set by Fuzzy Zoeller at the 1984 U.S. Open. There was a meeting of the clan near the top of the leaderboard. Aussie Robert Allenby had a share of the lead until a bogey at the final hole. Kite was among eight golfers at 68. The group included Greg Norman and Paul Stankowski, another candidate for the U.S. Ryder Cup team, along with Leonard.

Daly's performance was deja vu. He burst onto the scene at the PGA Championship in 1991 at Crooked Stick Golf Club in Carmel,

Indiana. He made it into the field as an alternate when Nick Price withdrew. Crooked Stick and Daly were the best example of the adage, "horses for courses." Daly was a perfect fit at the monstrously long Pete Dye design. He withered Crooked Stick with his awe-inspiring drives and wicked 180-yard short iron shots to win his first PGA Tour event. Four years later, Daly won the British Open at the Old Course at St. Andrews, a track so different from Crooked Stick it's amazing they're on the same planet. In between, Daly's behavior often bordered on otherwordly. His golf was obscured by personal problems, which included broken marriages and alcoholic addiction. But Big John was back at Winged Foot, at least for a little while.

"I'm always scared what's going to happen next so I don't want to get too excited," Daly said. "I'm just trying to keep my emotions level. Just try and stay at peace with myself...I believe I've had 15 chances in life. I'm scared of the disease. I'm scared of what it has done to me and what it can do to me. I guess I am scared to screw up again."

Daly's round included three straight birdies over Winged Foot's intimidating finishing holes — all par 4s measuring at least 448 yards. Woods was impressed.

"That's pretty awesome."

Woods hung around with another 70 in the second round and 71 in the third round, but his mood wasn't mellow Saturday night. He knew he had wasted an opportunity to do something more than just hang around.

Love and Leonard distanced themselves from the field in the third round. Love shot a second 66 and Leonard came along to break the course record with 65. Leonard's round was the kind that wins major championships. He hit every fairway, avoiding Winged Foot's Velcro rough, and made five birdies against no bogeys. "I think the round at The British Open was my best round; this was pretty close," Leonard said. In contrast, Woods needed Army fatigues.

Woods can execute shots no other golfer on the planet even considers. He's a throwback to the great shot-makers of yesteryear. He can rescue birdies from impossible places, as he did at the 16th hole at Winged Foot in the third round. But having that uncanny ability also makes it difficult for him to throttle back. His engine is always on full steam ahead. He will learn to be more discreet, but to suggest he should not explore the depth and width of his God-given talents is ridiculous. Greatness must be allowed to flourish.

"The Shot" at the 16th will be catalogued with the great shots in championship golf history. Here's the irony: It was also the shot that probably cost him any chance of winning the PGA Championship.

Woods kept hitting the ball into Winged Foot's beanstalk-tall rough, but he kept escaping and, remarkably, he was in position to challenge as he arrived on the 16th tee, a 457-yard par 4. There, he drove into the right rough between two oak trees. The ball was on a bare lie 171 yards from the flagstick. Woods' backswing was restricted and forced him to take the club up steeply. Somehow, he managed to get a 6-iron squarely onto the back of the ball and sent a high, slicing shot toward the green. It veered right like an airplane with a hydraulic system, landed just as smoothly, and rolled to a stop 12 feet from the hole. Woods made the putt to turn a bogey or worse into a birdie. It put him at 2-under-par and only 3 shots off the lead.

"I was just trying to get the ball in front of the green. That's all. It was one of those shots that came out perfect. That's all I can say about that. It flew a little further than I thought and got there."

At the next hole, Woods again drove into the rough. Again, he tried to play an impossible shot. Why not? He'd just pulled off a miracle and Woods is a momentum player. When he gets on a roll, his spirits soar and he plays off his success. His countenance is grimly noble. The demeanor is bulletproof. So he went for the green, taking another monumental swing out of the rough. The swing was so forceful it appeared Woods was trying to vaporize the golf course. Winged Foot has been around for more than 70 years. It's still there. Woods made double bogey and backed it up with a bogey at 18 (where he made a 10-foot putt to prevent another double). The comeback had gone awry, and Woods literally limped into the clubhouse.

"I hurt my ego — physically I'm fine. It was disappointing to finish the way I did and being right there, in contention, just 3 back

going into the final round and then do something that dumb. That's not what you want to do."

Double and triple bogeys were Woods' downfall in the three majors after The Masters. He made three double bogeys at Congressional, two triples and a quadruple bogey at Royal Troon, and the number continued to mount at Winged Foot.

"I thought I was very patient. I just hit too many bad shots and you can't afford to do that. I did make some mental errors, which cost me a couple of shots but overall I was very patient because you have to be. No choice. If you're not patient out here, it's going to show on this course."

Davis Love had been patiently waiting for his first major victory. When he arrived at Winged Foot for Sunday's final round, the temperature was searing. It was hot and humid, almost suffocating. When the mid-afternoon shower hit Mamaroneck, all that was left was the celebration — and the rainbow.

Love, poised to putt on the 18th green, glanced at the sky above and knew it was true. Like the song says, there is a rainbow connection and at the end of the rainbow there is a pot of gold.

Love's final putt, for birdie, followed the bend of a rainbow into the center of the cup. Love, 33, grew up in a golfing family and learned the game from his father, the respected player and teacher who was killed in a private airplane crash in 1988. For a decade, Love's pursuit was the most passionate and poignant in the sport. Love fired a final-round 66 for 269, 11 under par and 5 shots better than Leonard. The only other golfer under par was Lee Janzen, the 36-hole leader, at 279, 1 under.

"To win this championship is a great thrill for a son of a PGA member," Love said. "I'm in shock. Those last three, four holes were the hardest walk I've ever had trying to keep my composure. I was very comfortable with my golf game, but I was choking up a lot every time I thought what it would mean. I thought about my father. He played here in 1974 (U.S. Open) and he played in four or five PGA Championships. He'd be extremely pleased not only that I won a major but that it was the PGA Championship."

The words, and the scene, struck a chord with Woods.

"I had chills running up and down when he made that putt on 18 because I know some of the things that he shared with me about his dad. He can relate to the relationship I have with my dad. To see that rainbow — and it looked like the rainbow was going right where the hole was — and to see that ball go, you know that his dad said, 'That ball is going in.' To see him do that and share it with his family — his brother and his mom were there — that, to me, was everything, because he deserved it. He really does. He worked his butt off. He has had some bad breaks, but he has learned from them and it all paid off.

"I didn't make anything except for the putts I made on the last three holes. I needed to make some putts earlier in the round. The first hole is critical. I couldn't make it and that kind of set the tone for the whole day."

He hobbled around Winged Foot and admitted afterward that he had reinjured his left ankle the day before.

"It happened on the fourth hole. It's something I've been struggling with for a while."

The original injury was sustained during a break from his PGA Tour schedule following the British Open. Woods was asked if it was a factor in his performance.

"What do you think?"

The PGA Championship was Woods' first, and it marked the completion of the cycle for majors in 1997 for the young man who was supposed to challenge for the Grand Slam. Woods finished at 286, 6 over par, at Winged Foot to tie for 29th, his worst performance in a major. He was also 6 over at the U.S. Open, where he tied for 19th. He won The Masters with a 12-under 270 and was even par at the British and tied for 24th.

"It's been hectic — winning one, and after that the media surge. It was more than I expected. I thought that might happen down the road...not so soon. I am a little tired. The golf course wasn't easy. It beat all of us up except for Davis."

Shark Bait

NEC World Series of Golf
Firestone Country Club
Akron, Ohio
August 21–24

The first question out of the box at the NEC World Series of Golf concerned the Ryder Cup Matches. The anticipation was building. On Monday after the PGA Championship, Tom Kite, captain of the United States team, named his wild card selections. His choices were predictable. Fred Couples, when his head is in the game, remains one of the world's best golfers and certainly among the handful of most talented Americans. Lee Janzen's selection was less obvious. Janzen's form chart since 1995 — when he won three times — had been spotty, but he had played well at Winged Foot Golf Club and gutted it out in the final round. "I love my team," said Kite, who made it clear experience was the determining factor in his decisions. There were few dissenters, at least among Americans, that the 12-man squad was a powerhouse from top to bottom — from the No. 1 man, Tiger Woods, to the two captain's choices, Couples and Janzen.

"We needed to pick those two guys because, one, we don't have that much experience on our team. And they have been on Ryder Cups before and we need that kind of leadership. We have a captain who has been there many times — seven times — but we also need players to help out other players as well. And, when you are inside the ropes playing and partnering, it is nice to have a guy who has been there before who can help get you through."

The Ryder Cup was one of Woods' goals when he turned professional in 1996. He didn't talk about his personal expectations at the time, except to say he had goals and they were private, but there was little doubt that the Ryder Cup had to be on any short list. A student of golf history, Woods knows all about the Ryder Cup. Besides, after being on a team that lost the Walker Cup in Wales in 1996, he had plenty of incentive, a subject he talked about at length. Of course, there's also the match play element. Woods is a magnificent match player and the Ryder Cup puts him on the match play stage. Woods' length is intimidating, but so his short game. A golfer with one or the other has an edge going into match play. A golfer with both is mighty tough to beat. His three straight U.S. Amateur crowns attest to his ability in the format. To top it off, he's not just another pretty face. He's a grinder. He doesn't quit. He knows match play isn't about score. It's about the better golfer...and the better man. He's not shy about talking about it, either.

"I don't quit. I have no quit in me when I go out there and I'm down. I'm down but I'm not out. I'm not out until you close me out. And you always have to believe going into every single match that you play that you can win. Because sometimes you are going to get off to a bad start or [the opponent] can get off to a hot start and you can be down. You've got to believe in yourself, that you are going to win, that you are going to pull it out."

Woods arrived in Akron with a mind-set bordering on mixed emotions. He had regretted the decision to play at Westchester the week after the U.S. Open two months earlier.

"You never play a week after a major. Here I am again, but...this is different. This is a really big tournament and it is an honor to get in because you have to win to get in...I wish I would have played more at the beginning of the year because that is when you are most fresh. But, then again, I guess it paid off at Augusta because I was fresh."

Firestone Country Club is known for its length. Among the courses that appear annually on the PGA Tour schedule, Firestone is The

Monster. It's no surprise, therefore, that a Shark and a Tiger would be central characters on the 7,200-yard layout. Add some rain to soften the fairways and Firestone was playing even longer than usual. Certainly, that gave the advantage to long hitters.

Woods and Phil Mickelson, the defending champion, shot 67s to share the first-round lead in the select winners-only field of 46 golfers. Greg Norman — the Shark — was 1 shot behind along with Ernie "Big Cat" Els, Davis Love III, Nick Price, Mark O'Meara, and John Cook. The leaderboard was giving the first sellout crowd in the 22-year history of the World Series its money's worth. "It is a hard golf course and the best players seem to come out on a hard golf course," said Love, the newly-crowned PGA Champion. "I wasn't surprised to see Norman up there and won't be surprised to see Mickelson and Tiger. You know, this golf course kind of fits that style of golf. And except for Tiger, most of the guys on the leaderboard have played here quite a few times and are used to what it takes to play well on this course."

Mickelson made an early move. He was 4 under par after 11 holes before running into a bogey train. A long birdie putt at the home hole gave him a share of the lead. In contrast, Woods bogeyed the 18th or he would have had sole possession of the lead. He was able to shrug it off:

"I putted really well. I made some key putts to keep the round going. There are some putts that you need to make. I was able to make them and have some positive momentum going into the back nine. I made some good up-and-downs, as well. It feels pretty good because I played well today, and under these conditions, if you play well you are probably going to be up near the lead."

There was a Tiger sidebar at Firestone. His drive at the 16th didn't reach the forward tee markers. He hit it into the right rough, on the downslope of the ladies' tee.

"Hey, man, the ladies tees are way out there."

After a couple more skanks — a 4-iron that caromed off a cart path and a wedge that didn't threaten the green — he got it up-and-down from a greenside ridge for par. It was an aggressive play requiring a hard, spinning shot that had to die on the slope and trickle to the hole. The play inspired a birdie on the next hole, for a 2-shot lead, before the bogey at the last.

Woods and Mickelson matched scores again in Round II, but this time the number was 72 and it dropped them behind the new leader, Dudley Hart. Woods hit the ball all over Firestone, including a duck-hook into the gallery at the 9th hole. In two rounds, he hit only 11 fairways.

There was plenty of volatility on the leaderboard through 54 holes. Cook, the hometown boy, fired 67 to take a 1-shot lead over Mickelson, who tied the course record on the back nine with a 5-under-par 30 en route to 66. Norman was lurking in third place and Woods wasn't out of the hunt. He gritted out a 69 and was tied for fifth with David Ogrin and Englishman Lee Westwood.

"If I hit the ball just like I hit it today and make some putts, I'll be fine."

It was a Shark, not the Tiger, who took the biggest bite out of Firestone in Sunday's final round. Heavy rains soaked Firestone all week. On Sunday, it continued to rain, leaving puddles and streams everywhere, the sort of aquatic backdrop that would elevate the comfort level of any sea creature. Norman reeled off three birdies in a four-hole span on the back nine to lap the field for a 4-shot victory. He shot 3-under-par 67 to wipe out Cook's 2-shot lead.

Woods handled the conditions well enough to post a final round 70-278, 2 under par, and tie for third with Cook and Fred Funk. The $114,400 payday raised his season earnings to a record $1,949,920. It was his ninth top 10 finish and 13th top 25 in his 17 starts.

"It was brutal today. The rough was long and gnarly. The greens were pretty spikey. Those combinations are tough."

And there was a Great White Shark in the water.

September

Northern Exposure

Bell Canadian Open
Royal Montreal Golf Club
Montreal, Quebec, Canada
September 4–7

*I*t had to happen. Someday, Tiger Woods was bound to miss a cut as a professional. During Woods' early-season tear, the topic was fodder for grill room debates across America, and the inevitable conclusion was that when it happened it would make headlines.

Turns out that when it finally happened, it was so big it made headlines in two countries and in two languages.

It happened in Montreal, in the Province of Quebec, Canada's French-speaking enclave where separatists have been attempting for years to break away from the rest of the nation. Montreal, the city of churches, is the citadel of hockey. It is the home of the Montreal Canadiens, the greatest franchise in hockey history, and its legends like Maurice "The Rocket" Richard and Jean Beliveau, who once patrolled the ice at the hallowed Montreal Forum with the elegance and dignity of a world leader. Hockey is a birthright in Canada. Offspring are bred to skate, to shoot, to score, and someday don the jersey of a championship hockey team. The summer season is short in Quebec but golf is hugely popular in the province.

Tiger Woods doesn't play hockey. His birthright is golf. Good thing. He isn't adept at skating on thin ice, and he was never steady on his feet at Royal Montreal Golf Club. Unsuccessful at the U.S. and British Opens, Woods saw the Canadian Open as a chance to add a national title to his 1997 haul.

"A national Open is always a big deal."

The weather in Montreal was more befitting the start of hockey training camp than a golf tournament. It was 10 degrees — on the Celsius scale. But that's still only about 50 degrees Fahrenheit.

On any scale, it was cold, and so was Woods' game.

So cold, in fact, that caddies were bracing for snow.

The subject of golf paparazzi came up several times during the week, with the Canadian Open starting just days after the death of Princess Diana in an automobile accident in Paris. It was a logical topic. Woods had been chased across continents by photographers and media and his profile was reaching royal proportions. Few athletes anywhere are more in demand or more sought after.

"I've had threats to my life, but not from the press pushing me to the limit. I'll keep on being me. But the tragedy that happened shows that something will have to be done about the press being as aggressive as they are. When you chase after people and cause people to lose their lives, you have to take a long and serious look at it.

"I think it happens to royalty, movie stars, and Hollywood figures. Our living is made in public. They see us all the time. Royalty and stars don't work in public as much, so when they do come out, people want to see them."

The galleries at Royal Montreal, where the flags were flying at half mast, didn't get to see much of Woods. He was gone after 36 holes.

Woods opened with a 70 but there were early signs that the second round would be different. Woods started with a triple bogey 7. Needing just to par in to make the cut, he made three bogeys on the final four holes, for 76-146, 1 shot above the cut line. It ended his string of 25 cuts made.

Royal Montreal was set up for a major championship. The dogleg fairways were narrow, the rough long. At the first hole, Woods chipped three times — short, long and, finally, on — and then two-putted. He started the hole by driving into the rough, and then missed the green. It added up to another big number, the kind that had been so telling in his failed bids at the U.S. Open, the British Open, and the

PGA Championship, where statisticians had taken to computing his scores of double bogey or higher. Including the Canadian, the count was 11, for a total of 27 over par.

Woods made bogey at the 15th and 16th holes, but steadied the ship with a dramatic 25-foot birdie putt on the 17th. He seemed poised to make the cut and extend the streak.

"I knew when I saw the leaderboard walking off the 16th green that I needed a birdie."

All he needed at the 18th was a par. He couldn't make it. His downfall started with a drive that found the rough and he couldn't get his second shot on the green. His 20-foot putt to save par just missed. Woods was philosophical.

"It had to happen. I can't play my entire career without missing a cut."

Pillars of Hercules

The Ryder Cup
Valderrama Golf Club
Sotogrande, Spain
September 26–28

*T*he Costa del Sol is Spain's sun coast, where the weather is idyllic and the travel brochures insist rain is only a rumor. Presumably, that's where we get the line about the rain in Spain falling mainly in the plain. It never rains on the coastal villages of the Mediterranean Sea, except when it pours. If you're looking for omens to explain the demise of the United States Ryder Cup Team in September 1997, there were plenty of black clouds lingering around Sotogrande. As it turned out, the rain in Spain was falling mainly on 12 American golfers and their captain. The first day of competition on Friday, September 26, was delayed by early morning storms moving up from North Africa. Converging weather patterns produced winds with the force of warp speeds crashing off the Mediterranean, and the heavy rains that flooded the area.

The Ryder Cup, on its 70th anniversary, was being held for the first time on mainland Europe. The man responsible was Seve Ballesteros, the European captain whose debut in the matches nearly two decades earlier had changed the face of the competition. In 1979, Ballesteros and fellow Spaniard Antonio Garrido became the first continental players to join the Great Britain side in the Ryder Cup. The inclusion, and the subsequent arrival of Germany's Bernhard Langer, Spain's José María Olazabal, the new breed Swedes, and others, helped level the scales, and suddenly the Europeans became a match for the Americans. In fact, they were beating the Americans more often than they were losing to the red, white, and blue.

The record stood at 3-2-1, in favor of Europe, over the six matches preceding Valderrama. Ballesteros was the heart, soul, and inspiration of the European team as a player. His reward was a Ryder Cup in his native Spain, and the captaincy. Seve was no longer a player in Spain. His game had gone south, a transition that had started even before the 1995 Ryder Cup Matches at Oak Hill Country Club in Rochester, New York. There was considerable speculation that Ballesteros, a master at match play, would put himself on the team if his game recovered in time. It didn't. Not even close. So Ballesteros had a new role at Valderrama. He was Europe's conscience.

Like yachting's America's Cup, the Ryder Cup was an esoteric spectacle and had been unimportant in the general scheme of things for much of its existence. Nobody much cared. It was an exercise in sportsmanship, just as its founder, Samuel Ryder, an English seed merchant, had hoped when he put up the solid gold cup. His intention was that golf professionals from Great Britain and the United States should meet every two years in a friendly competition promoting goodwill.

But the Americans were so dominant that the Ryder Cup became an embarrassment. The British team was expanded to include Great Britain and Ireland and, in 1979, golfers from continental Europe. Between 1935 and 1983, the British, GBI, and European entries won just once, in 1957, in Yorkshire, England. In 1985, with Ballesteros leading the way, the Ryder Cup finally returned to Europe.

In 1987, Europe won for the first time ever on American soil — at Jack Nicklaus' Muirfield Village Golf Club in Dublin, Ohio — and retained the Cup two years later in England, when the competition wound up in a 14-14 tie. In the event of a tie, the holder retains the goldware.

As the battle heated up, literally and figuratively, people began to notice. With increased interest and exposure, the Ryder Cup began to emerge as an important competition in golf. Competition is the operative word. As the sides really began to compete, it was often at the expense of the sportsmanship and camaraderie Samuel Ryder had envisioned as his purpose for the Ryder Cup. But that had been less a problem the past couple of renewals. With the Europeans growing stronger, the attention from both sides was on winning the Cup, not the war.

It was the Europeans who were doing the trash talking on the eve of the Ryder Cup '97. Emboldened by their local knowledge at Valderrama, site of the European PGA Tour's Volvo Masters, they spouted off, and most of the darts were aimed at Tiger Woods, the young star of the American team and Ryder Cup rookie.

Ballesteros said, "Any of my 12 men are willing to compete with Tiger Woods and can beat Tiger Woods."

Ian Woosnam, who had never won a singles match in Ryder Cup competition and couldn't find an Augusta fairway with a marble, boasted, "Give me Tiger in the last match on the last day and I'll whip his butt, as the Americans say."

Colin Montgomerie, the Scot who was bombed by Woods at Augusta National, chimed in, too. Montgomerie, coming off an exceptional final round 63 at the British Masters, took the opportunity to challenge Woods. "I'll take anybody, anytime, around Valderrama," Montgomerie said. "But Tiger's the one we all want to play because we've got nothing to lose." It was Montgomerie who had said some months earlier that Woods' presence on the team gave the United States a 5-0 head start.

At Augusta National, Woods routed a field that included European Ryder Cup members Woosnam, Montgomerie, Nick Faldo, Bernhard Langer, Costantino Rocca, José María Olazabal, Lee Westwood, and the captain, Ballesteros. But, as Montgomerie confidently pointed out, Valderrama isn't Augusta National.

"I'd not fancy playing [Woods] at Augusta," Montgomerie said. "But we're playing Valderrama, which isn't a course that suits him, whereas my record there is pretty good."

Montgomerie also made reference to Brad Faxon's divorce, suggesting that with such pressing personal things on his mind, Faxon would be ineffective in the matches. Montgomerie went on to say Scott Hoch's history of missing short putts made him vulnerable in the heat of the Ryder Cup.

Woods, and the other Americans, didn't engage in the repartee.

"I've played enough match play, I should be OK. I always prefer match play over medal any day. Match play is the epitome, one-on-one. Anyone can win in match play. That's what makes it so great. There's so much emotion. You ride the wave [of emotion]...it's neat."

Woods was asked by the European press if saying that "anyone can win in match play" was an admission of weakness.

"It's true. They can beat me. But, vice versa, we've got 12 guys on this side who can beat any of their guys. That's the great thing. That's why we're coming together Friday. We're going to find out."

Tom Kite, the U.S. captain, and his golfers were playing good cop to Europe's bad cop. The Americans didn't utter a controversial syllable. They were perfect guests. They said and did the right things. But the failure by veteran Americans to respond to the comments by Montgomerie, Woosnam, and Ballesteros directed at Woods raised eyebrows in the press tent. Nobody said, "You guys want Tiger, you've got to go through me to get at him," or similar words reflecting a fighting spirit. The best line, as usual, would come out of the press tent a few days later when the pairings for the opening Fourball (best ball) matches were announced.

The pairings for the Ryder Cup competition are a blind draw. In each format, the captains put their two-man teams together and list them, 1 through 4, without knowing in what order the opposition will place its teams. It's been suggested that an obvious way to improve the competition, make it even better than it is, and put more emphasis on a captain's role at the same time is to allow them to match the teams. For instance, Ballesteros would name his No. 1 Foursomes (alternate shot) team and Kite would be allowed to assign one of his teams to play against it. Next, Kite would announce his No. 2 team, and Ballesteros would have the opportunity — taking into consideration relative strengths and weaknesses of the golfers — to put his team of choice against Kite's pair. The captains could put style against style, strength against strength, superstars against superstars.

In singles, each captain lists his players from 1 to 12 and each golfer faces the corresponding number among the opposition. There is no strategy. Just dumb luck. So, it was easy for the Europeans to talk about wanting Tiger Woods in singles. The odds were against them and they knew it. Only one man could draw Tiger. Besides, Montgomerie was spot-on when he said they would have nothing to lose against Wonder Boy. Nobody would expect a victory over Tiger Woods. If it happened, it would be a glorious triumph and heralded throughout the golf-playing world.

࿇

There were controversies on both sides of the Atlantic Ocean as the Ryder Cup Matches neared. In Europe, the dismissal of Miguel Ángel Martín from a spot he rightfully earned made headlines. Martín, a Spaniard, suffered a wrist injury in midsummer. Although Martín insisted he would be ready for Valderrama, Ballesteros removed him from the team. Martín, who held down the 10th and final spot on the European points list, was replaced by No. 11 José María Olazabal.

It was a convenient circumstance for Ballesteros. A European team without Olazabal was a weaker team, and since Ballesteros' long-time Ryder Cup partner — they were known as the Spanish Armada — didn't qualify on points, it was necessary to put him on the team. By replacing Martín with Olazabal, it still left Ballesteros two wild card selections, which he used to select Nick Faldo and Jesper Parnevik. Controversy or not, Ballesteros' team had come together just as he had envisioned. The rest he didn't have time to worry about. The Martín expulsion was a minor distraction for Seve. He was running the ship, and nobody — certainly not Miguel Ángel Martín — was going to incite a mutiny.

Tiger Woods finally met President Clinton in a hastily arranged bon voyage for some of the American players. It occurred in a New York hotel, and the discussion didn't revolve around golf as much as it did Chelsea Clinton, the president's daughter, who was off to college at Stanford. The President and the First Lady, Hillary Rodham Clinton, had helped Chelsea get settled into her dormitory a couple of days earlier. Woods, of course, also attended Stanford for two years before turning professional. The president was in New York attending a United Nations function and the U.S. team — Captain Tom Kite and those members who weren't already in Europe or en route — gathered in the Big Apple for the trip, by Concorde, to Spain.

Earl Woods wasn't in the traveling party. Therein was an American controversy. In an interview published by an English newspaper, Tiger's dad blasted the Professional Golfers' Association of America for not allowing Tiger to have a second seat on the Concorde or an inside-the-ropes pass. Each member of the team is allowed to take a spouse or significant other on the Concorde. That person also gets to walk the fairways with the players and officials. Earl Woods argued that since Tiger had no wife or girlfriend, that spot should go to Kultida or Earl Woods. The truth is, Earl Woods had a strong argument, but the PGA of America didn't see it that way. Earl said he would protest by staying home in California.

Access to the golfers is limited at the Ryder Cup. There are several reasons. Among them is the crush of activities. The golfers are shepherded around to various functions which occupy virtually all of their waking hours. There's something going on all the time — gala banquets, dignitaries and royalty to acknowledge (former President George Bush and Barbara Bush, the King and Queen of Spain, Prince Andrew, and the crown prince of basketball, Michael Jordan, for starters), and ceremonies.

The opening ceremonies Thursday featured Andalusian show horses in a never-ending display of equestrian entertainment. A British commentator said the 2 hours and 40 minutes of festivities verged on the absurd. Upon returning to the United States, Woods would comment on the large number of functions the golfers were required to attend, saying it was no way to get ready for a major tournament.

The players are made available to the media in pairs of two on Tuesday and Wednesday. The captains are available formally each day. Otherwise, it's catch-as-catch-can. Some of the golfers don't mind spending a few minutes with the media; others avoid it. Woods' partner for the formal interrogation Tuesday afternoon was Tom Lehman.

There were no revelations, with the Americans sticking to their nonconfrontational mode. Woods talked about how much he'd grown up in the past 12 months, how 1997 was the longest year of his life, and how much he'd looked forward to someday playing in the Ryder Cup. He found the perfect analogy in terms Europeans could understand for the nationalism and partisanship the Ryder Cup engenders: Soccer.

"It's been a long year, but to have it finally come around to something I've seen on TV since I was a little boy and I've wanted to experience...to have people root against you, be really harsh, I think that's kind of cruel. You don't see it very often in golf. It's like being in a different sport. It's like baseball, football, or especially soccer, where people are rooting against you and it's something I've always wanted to come over here and experience."

His teammates were delighted to have Woods among them. "I think everyone is excited that Tiger is on this team," Kite said. "Not only the players on my team but the players on the European team. Certainly, I think it's to be expected that everyone would like to have a shot at him. I know when I played my first Ryder Cup in 1979, I drew Tony Jacklin. I loved it. Tony was one of the top players and I drew him in the singles and I was very excited about it. So I can see why those players would like to draw Tiger."

Mark O'Meara, who would partner with Woods in the opening match Friday, looked for big things from Tiger. "He's an unbelievable talent and he'll adapt to any situation," O'Meara said. "He's hitting the ball well. He's excited. I would expect Tiger to play quite well this week."

Lehman told the audience what he had previously told Woods privately. "He's handled himself incredibly well this year," Lehman said. "I'm proud to be on the same team with Tiger this week. He's one of the guys."

The clubhouse at Valderrama looks like a contemporary Alamo. The landscape, the coloring, and the architecture of the region resemble the southwestern United States. Like the Alamo, the clubhouse is a maze of entrances and corridors. In retrospect, perhaps the Alamo isn't the best analogy.

Tiger Woods stood at the top of the first set of steps at the main portal. He turned left, then right, and then squared up again. He knew where the driving range was located but he wasn't quite sure how to get there.

"Which way?"

Fluff Cowan stepped in. "I've got a great idea," the caddie said. "Why don't you follow me instead of me following you." A few moments later, they were at the range, where Germany's Bernhard Langer was already hitting long irons. The fans in the bleachers "oohed" and "aahed" as Woods hit a few wedges before starting the move up through the bag. His action was pure. The crowd loved it. So did Mark O'Meara, who walked over to Woods and Cowan and said, "Glad you're my partner today."

Woods and O'Meara played with Lee Janzen and Scott Hoch. Woods, who visited Valderrama in July for a first look, played smoothly. At the 535-yard par 5 4th hole, Woods crushed a tee shot. All he had left to the green was a 5-iron and he landed it 12 feet from the pin.

"It's just not fair, is it?" Janzen said, and the gallery howled with delight.

"It's a par 5 for three of us, anyway," Hoch offered.

Kite used Woods with various partners in practice. When Woods teed it up with Phil Mickelson in a group that included Davis Love III and Fred Couples, it led to speculation that since Love and Couples were an established pairing, Woods and Mickelson would also become a partnership. The theory was that Woods and Mickelson, playing on his second Ryder Cup team after going 3-0 at Oak Hill, were sure to be mainstays of the U.S. team for the next decade at least, and this was as good a time as any to put them together. The anticipation was that Woods and Mickelson would be the reincarnation of the

Spanish Armada — Ballesteros and Olazabal — a virtually unbeatable pair that would guarantee the Americans an important block of Ryder Cup points every two years.

"I have some good ideas...strong possibilities," Kite said. "I've got quite a few possibilities for Tiger and more for O'Meara."

Valderrama is a wonderful golf course. It was designed by Robert Trent Jones in 1979, with some renovations 14 years later, and there isn't a golf course anywhere in the world — this side of Augusta National — that is in any better condition than Valderrama. That's the reason it is revered as the Augusta National of Europe — not the design features, because those are not similar. Augusta is wide, with expansive fairways, everything on a grand scale, with no rough. Augusta is a driver's delight, as Woods proved in April.

Valderrama requires precision over power off the tee. Cork oak trees line the fairways and, in a few instances, intrude into the middle of the fairways (as on the 2nd hole) or block the entrances into greens. That's what Colin Montgomerie was talking about when he said Valderrama did not suit Woods' game but rather his own. Montgomerie is known as a long, straight driver of the golf ball.

Another controversy at Valderrama was Ballesteros' redesign of the 17th hole. Depending on who you ask, it's either the worst hole in Europe...or the best. To take the comparisons to Augusta to the next level, Ballesteros took great pains to design the green complex at the 17th in the image of Augusta National's two back nine par 5s, the 13th and the 15th. "It looks like they took the 13th and 15th greens at Augusta and combined them," Jeff Maggert said. "The hole doesn't fit the style of the rest of the course...[but] it's an interesting hole."

Kite didn't attach much significance to the design features. "It's not for me to approve or disapprove — the golf course is what it is," he said. "I think it's a wonderful golf course. I like it very much. It's unique, tight, fairly tricky. It's a great golf course for match play." That's because there are so many variables and a daunting finish where matches can change dramatically.

The 17th hole — a par 5 of 511 yards — has a green guarded on the front and left by a pond. Ballesteros added mounds in the first landing area, which ends with an apron of rough beyond 290 yards. The rough stretches about 20 yards before there is more fairway. The mounds are criticized because they can knock even the straightest drive off-line and into the rough. The rough is even more question-able because it penalizes anybody who can drive the ball more than 290 yards and straight. Did somebody say Tiger Woods, Davis Love III, Phil Mickelson, and Fred Couples all in the same breath?

From the rough which bisects the fairway, it's a layup second shot with a wedge and a wedge approach to the very slick, very slanted green. The banks of the putting surfaces are closely shaved — an-other Augusta National trait — and balls that are even slightly off-line have nothing to stop them from going into the pond. Birdie attempts can become double bogeys faster than a flamenco dancer can tap.

"It's the worst hole we play all year," Montgomerie said. "I know who designed it [Ballesteros] and I don't care. He may be the best player whoever lived, but he's no course designer."

Ballesteros' answer: "If you don't like the hole, win your matches 3-and-2."

If the tabloids are an indication of who's hot, then Tiger Woods was the hottest man in Spain. The British tabloids were full of Woods, with *The Sun* carrying four photos of the phenom and a headline: "Raging Tiger is just a spoilt brat and cry baby...says golf guru Mac O'Grady." Whose guru O'Grady is, it didn't say. The story read, in part: "The smile is worth more than $100 million...but temper and aloofness have left Woods friendless, an attitude irritating more and more of his fellow pros." It quoted O'Grady on Tiger, when O'Grady on Ballesteros might have been an even better story. O'Grady helped Ballesteros with his swing a few years ago before that partnership broke up. O'Grady is quoted on Woods: "When he is playing well, the beautiful smile shows and his dreams fly. But when he doesn't he crashes down to earth like an F-14 doing 2,000 mph." Now the best part: The story went on to say Woods "doesn't have the serenity of Faldo."

Of course, that would be Nick Faldo, who left his homeland of England and the European Tour to get as far away from the British tabloids as he could and still be in a part of the civilized world. The tabloids made Faldo's life hell and the serenity they now spoke about came only because he left. But still, to describe the twice-divorced Faldo, whose second marriage broke up at the 1995 Ryder Cup, as serene was simply a figment of tabloid imagination. When Faldo's involvement with a young American co-ed was discovered, she, too, became the subject of screaming headlines in England. The tabloids dispatched reporters to track her down, to stalk her, and go through her garbage looking for evidence of her relationship to Faldo. To this day, Faldo is on his guard near the tabloid media. His interviews end abruptly when tabloid reporters arrive.

Seve Ballesteros was first into the interview area Thursday afternoon to announce his teams, and order of play, for the next day's opening Fourball matches. José María Olazabal and Costantino Rocca; Nick Faldo and Lee Westwood; Jesper Parnevik and Per-Ulrik Johansson; and Colin Montgomerie and Bernhard Langer.

Moments later, Tom Kite unveiled his teams. Davis Love III and Phil Mickelson would go off first, followed by Fred Couples and Brad Faxon. The third pairing was Tom Lehman and Jim Furyk. The words didn't come out of Kite's mouth fast enough. Everybody knew what was next. Tiger Woods would be in the fourth slot. His partner was Mark O'Meara. And, in the blind draw, their opponents for Friday morning were Colin Montgomerie and Bernhard Langer. Tiger vs. Montgomerie. Greg Stoda of the *Palm Beach Post* didn't miss a beat. "Tiger should go up to Montgomerie and say, 'OK, Fatass, you got me. What are you going to do with me?'" The press contingent howled. The stage was set for the most anticipated Ryder Cup in history.

♋♋

The storm off the coast of North Africa slammed into the Costa del Sol with a vengeance Friday morning at about 5 A.M. It knocked out power lines, flooded homes, soaked Valderrama, and delayed the scheduled 9 A.M. start of the 1997 Ryder Cup nearly three hours.

There is more pressure on the first tee at the Ryder Cup than any endeavor in sports. The worst part is waiting, and when the wait is extended three hours, after days of anticipation, the experience can become gruesome. "Nothing comes close to it, really," said Lee Westwood, the English rookie who was to play alongside Nick Faldo.

When Tiger Woods and Mark O'Meara walked through the ropes behind the first tee for the match against Montgomerie and Langer, three games were already on the course. The Americans were off to a good start and now the anchor team was getting ready.

Four Americans were not scheduled to play Friday morning. Lee Janzen, Justin Leonard, Jeff Maggert, and Scott Hoch accompanied their teammates from the putting green to the first tee. They offered encouragement and support while trying not to get in the way. When Janzen stepped onto the first tee, there were six American journalists already inside the ropes. One of them turned to Janzen and said, "Think Tiger will go up to Montgomerie and say, 'OK, Fatass, you got me, now what are you going to do with me?'"

Janzen shook his head. "No, Tiger would never say anything like that," Janzen said. "What he's got to say he'll say with his clubs."

Woods stepped up to the tee, nodded acknowledgement of his introduction, took a mighty swing and lashed the ball down the middle of the first fairway at Valderrama.

"Yes, there was pressure. I wasn't as nervous as I thought I would be. When I stepped up to the first tee I was pretty nervous. Once I finished the first hole I was all right again. I was psyched."

Montgomerie and Langer, both winners of the Volvo Masters at Valderrama, did not make a birdie in the match. "It was embarrassing," Montgomerie admitted. The Americans were steady if not spectacular, and won, 3-and-2. The match was all square through three holes. Woods made birdie at the fourth, with former President Bush and Barbara Bush watching at greenside. A par 3 at the 6th was good for a 2-up lead, which grew at the 10th when Woods made his second birdie of the match.

It ended when O'Meara, embracing his role as the veteran in the partnership, knocked in a 30-foot birdie putt at the 16th. "This year's Ryder Cup is a little different," said O'Meara, a member of the team for the fourth time. "I'm a little older and have a lot more experience, but the pressure is just the same. I truly enjoyed playing with Tiger."

Couples and Faxon also produced a victory for the United States, and the Fourball matches ended all square, at 2 points each.

Kite sent the four men who didn't play in the morning Fourballs — Janzen, Hoch, Leonard, and Maggert — out for the first two Foursomes games in the afternoon. They were followed by Lehman and Mickelson. The only tandem remaining intact was Woods–O'Meara. Once again, Montgomerie and Langer were the opponents. The only difference was the format. Foursomes is alternate shot, something the Americans never play. Advantage: Europe.

Woods and O'Meara were 2-down after three holes and never led the match. After the Americans won the 4th hole with a birdie, there was a huge turning point in favor of the Europeans. They won the 8th and 9th holes with birdies. A par would have won the 7th hole for the Americans.

"They were going to make bogey at seven and we had a chance and didn't get it done," O'Meara said. "I left Tiger short on the first putt on eight. On nine, Tiger hit a perfect tee shot. I had a 4-iron to the green. They had a 2-iron and hit it to within about eight feet and made birdie. We made par. We have respect for their game. They have respect for our game. Colin didn't play very well in the morning, then played a lot better in the afternoon. They just didn't make many mistakes this afternoon." The score: Europe 5-and-3.

Montgomerie and Langer both made adjustments after the morning defeat. Langer switched putters, going to a center-shafted long putter. Montgomerie worked on his swing. He tried to get more extension through impact. The alternate shot match ended at the 15th, where Langer's approach shot left Montgomerie a 17-foot putt for birdie and the victory. He knocked it in. "I had to hole that putt for him (Langer)," Montgomerie said. "I loved it."

Woods' game was sporadic on Day One.

"In the afternoon, we didn't hit the ball as good as we would have liked and we didn't make the putts. That's the key, and Colin turned his game around completely. I've got to give him credit for that. He played great. And Bernhard was as rock steady as ever."

The rain delay pushed two of the Foursomes matches into Saturday morning. The outcome of those would be critical, since the other two had been split, with Hoch and Janzen producing a big victory over Olazabal and Rocca, 1-up. The Americans didn't fare well in the suspended matches. Europe earned a victory and a half for a 4½ to 3½ lead.

᧞᧞

*B*loody Saturday.

Day Two had an ominous beginning. Again, the skies were dark and there was rain. There was also a bad start — a mere half-point from the suspended matches — to contend with. It would get worse. Much worse.

The Europeans muscled up on the unsuspecting Americans. There was a rout in the making. There are 12 golfers, plus a captain, on each side, but it was clear Saturday that the U.S. was being double-teamed. The Europeans won 3½ points in the morning, and 2½ in the afternoon, which again spilled over into the next day.

In too many cases, the Americans had only one effective golfer, while the Europeans paired up perfectly. There was no better example than the Justin Leonard–Brad Faxon match against Welshman Ian Woosnam and Dane Thomas Bjorn. Leonard, the 25-year-old British Champion, eagled the 4th when he holed an 83-yard wedge from the fairway on the par 5 and followed with birdies at the 5th and 6th holes. He also birdied the 9th and 10th. Despite an outbound 30 — 5 under par — the Americans were beaten.

Leonard cooled off on the back, but Faxon wasn't there to pick up the slack. "Justin Leonard did everything to win," Woosie said. "It's nerve and battle...whether you've got it or not. The U.S. has a very good team — a very good lineup — but that doesn't matter when it comes to match play."

Bjorn, a Ryder rookie, said, "Ian played great at the beginning. I played lovely in the middle of the round and then we both played quite well at the end. We did what we had to do in Fourball. One of us was in there all of the time and we put a lot of pressure on the

Americans. Justin just didn't get the support from Faxon." The match score was 2-and-1.

Playing well was no consolation for Leonard. "You don't get points for playing well.... One or both [of the Europeans] is always in the hole."

Nick Faldo's partnership with Lee Westwood provided the same kind of dependency and the same result. They beat Tiger Woods and Mark O'Meara, 2-and-1.

"If I can do the solid stuff, [Westwood] knows he has a par standing on the tee," Faldo said. "On this course, especially, both have to be in the hole."

Westwood made five birdies, including three straight beginning at the 9th, and Faldo contributed three. Woods and O'Meara each made three birdies.

"Westwood played some superb golf," O'Meara said. "We were 2-up going to the 9th. Tiger hit it in there pretty close (20 feet) and had a chance for birdie. Westwood made it from about 25 feet and Tiger didn't make his. That was a major swing hole for us."

"If I'd have made that putt, it might have been a different story. I didn't play that badly. I hit it as well as I hit it the entire week. Lee played unbelievably well. I had a chance to top him at nine. I didn't do it and he got on a roll. He birdied the next two holes and kept hitting it stiff."

The match ended when Woods' eagle putt at the par 5 17th ran off the green and into the water. Even the intensely partisan gallery was stunned by the awkward attempt. Woods had been hardened and prepared for the anti-American sentiments by his experience at the British Open at Royal Troon.

"It's kind of neat, actually. I'm surprised at how many Americans are over here cheering for us — and we really appreciate it."

When the afternoon Foursomes began, Kite and his team knew they were up against a rock and a hard place. When the alternate shot matches were finally completed Sunday morning, the U.S. was down 5 points. They would have had a better chance defending

Gibraltar against the Moorish invasion than they did rebounding against the Europeans.

Kite sent Woods and Leonard out in the third alternate shot match against Jesper Parnevik and Antonio Garrido. Neither side was ever more than 1-up. The Americans struck first, with a birdie on the opening hole, before the match eventually spilled over to Sunday morning.

It was all square at the 17th, where Leonard, hitting the second shot in the alternate format after a Woods drive, lasered a 1-iron to the back right of the green. The Americans needed two putts for birdie and a 1-up lead. Woods studied the 45-foot downhill putt. Parnevik, watching closely, knew about the putt by Woods that had skated off the same green the previous day. He didn't expect another aberration from Woods. But the putt wouldn't stop this time, either. It rolled some 20 feet past the cup and Leonard could not convert the birdie. Parnevik took a deep breath and knocked in his six-foot putt to halve the hole.

"Tiger and I both played well," Leonard said. "They made a few more putts. We had a couple of chances at the last two holes and weren't able to take advantage of it. We both would have loved to get a full point, but we'll take anything we can get at this point."

"It was a great match. Garrido made some key putts and then Parnevik made a key putt on 17 after I blew it past the hole. We hit a lot of good shots and so did they and it ended up a halve.

"I'm feeling a lot of pressure. There is a lot of pressure out there. I felt it on the first day. I felt it on the second day and now on the third day. It's definitely out there because you are not only playing for yourself, you're playing for your teammates and your country."

On Saturday morning, the United States had led all four bestball matches on the back nine, and won none. Only the Lehman–Mickelson partnership produced a halve. When the Americans had the lead, they squandered it. The Europeans ruled supreme on the greens.

"Looks like you all are shell-shocked, too," Kite said in the interview room. "We started out strong and the momentum was on our side. As they have all week, they've played much better on the back nine than we did. For what reason, I'm not exactly sure.... They're severely out-putting us."

"It's not insurmountable," the captain said. "We're going to have to play like crazy but it's not insurmountable."

As he left the interview area, Kite tried to think of something to say at the team dinner. "I was at a loss for words," he admitted. Instead, he sought out former President Bush, an avid golfer and enthusiastic supporter of the U.S. team. Kite was aware that the ex-president was staying at the home of Jaime Ortiz-Patino — the owner of Valderrama — whose mansion is on the golf course.

Kite knew what had to be done — he had to get the ex-president to talk to the team. "I intercepted him before he made it to the dinner, and with Jimmy Patino's blessing we delayed his arrival by some 40 or 45 minutes," Kite said. The American golfers were in the team room having dinner. They were pleased to see the ex-president and, according to Kite, gave him an "enthusiastic welcome."

"It wasn't important what [the ex-president] said but that he was there for us," the captain said. "He did a great job."

Valderrama Golf Club is just a few miles from the Rock of Gibraltar, one of mythology's two pillars of Hercules. On a clear day, the Rock rises majestically. The view from the controversial 17th fairway is awesome.

The Americans needed a Herculean effort in the singles to bounce back from a 5-point deficit. Since Fred Couples, Davis Love, Tiger Woods, and Justin Leonard had to complete their suspended matches Sunday morning, Kite's strategy was to put them off first in singles instead of having them finish in the morning, then wait, then go through the entire warm-up routine again.

The tactic made sense for another reason. Kite had to load up early in an attempt to get back into the fray. The United States needed some victories at the top to put pressure on the Europeans. After those four, he came right back with Phil Mickelson and Mark O'Meara. Only Tom Lehman was saved, and he went last in the event the 12th game mattered. It didn't. The rock solid Lehman was off the course early with his 7-and-6 rout of Antonio Garrido.

"We knew we had to get off to a good start," Kite said. "I had six players on the golf course but Jeff [Maggert] and Scott [Hoch] only had four holes to go so they were going to have to experience a little cool-down anyway. The way the time was working, it looked like Freddie, Davis, Tiger, and Justin were going to time it pretty well so they could finish up their round and with a very short time in between be able to flip around."

Couples drew Ian Woosnam; Love got Per-Ulrik Johansson; Woods was matched against Costantino Rocca; and Leonard went out against Thomas Bjorn. Seve Ballesteros saved his big guns for later. There was to be no Woods–Montgomerie match, or Woods–Faldo.

In Costantino Rocca, the good-natured Italian, the Europeans had found the perfect opponent for Woods. A veteran who twice before had lost important singles matches to Davis Love III in the Ryder Cup, Rocca isn't the kind to fuel any fires. He's a pleasant chap. The American supporters in the galleries would find it hard to cheer against Rocca — they would have had no trouble doing so if the opponent were Montgomerie or Faldo or Westwood or Olazabal.

Couples was ablaze against Woosnam, who had wanted Woods but had to settle instead for Boom Boom. In the singles match at Valderrama, Couples was a Sonic Boom. He routed Woosnam, 8-and-7. In 11 holes, Couples had five birdies and an eagle to tie the Ryder Cup record for largest margin of victory in singles. It matched the record held by Tom Kite, in 1989, against Howard Clark.

The Americans needed to continue the momentum established by Couples' decisive victory. Davis Love III won the first hole with a birdie against Per-Ulrik Johansson but never won another. With the match all square through 12 holes, Johansson won the next three holes and the match, 3-and-2.

Next on the course were Tiger Woods and Costantino Rocca, the man who had been conquered by 6 shots in the final round at Augusta National. The gallery supporting Rocca wore tee shirts that proclaimed, "The Rocca of Gilbraltar." He was every bit as sturdy and majestic against the young American.

Woods never led in the match after Rocca opened with a birdie 3 at the first hole. In fact, Woods made only one birdie and won only one hole — both at the 11th. Rocca went 3-up through five as Woods failed even to birdie the par 5 4th hole. The 9th hole was a microcosm of the match. There, on the 441-yard par 4, Rocca drilled a 22-foot par putt. That left Woods with about a 4-foot putt for the halve. Woods missed, and Rocca went 4-up after shooting 32 on the outward nine to Tiger's birdie-less 37.

"It was a big putt if I could somehow make it. I had a little 3- or 4-footer, down the hill. He holed his and I missed. Instead of having a putt to win the hole I had to try to halve the hole and I missed, so I end up losing the hole. That was a big momentum breaker. I was trying to build and claw myself back into the match and it just didn't work."

Rocca, the veteran, knew what had to be done the rest of the way. He simply could not leave any openings, and he didn't. As Rocca made par after par — 11 straight — Woods needed birdies to win and there was only one.

When Seve Ballesteros caught up with the match at the 16th hole, it was all but over. Woods had missed his approach shot to the right. Ballesteros saw that Rocca was in a difficult situation, in trees. Rocca, with a cushion to fall back on, chose the dynamic play — a low, screaming 1-iron that made the green. "It was like one of Seve's shots," the Italian said.

"I just saw his lie — it was OK. I wanted to see what kind of lie he had and whether he was going to pitch out or not. My shot was important to put heat on him and I didn't quite do that. This gave him an opportunity to freewheel it and see if he could pull off a miracle shot. He pulled it off. It was unbelievable. It was a low-cut 1-iron. It was a gutsy shot and he pulled it off."

Rocca and Woods shook hands on the 16th green, where Rocca's par gave him the hole and the match, 4-and-2. "I came here to play for the team, not myself," Rocca said.

"It's called golf. You can't always win. All you can hope for is that things go your way. You go out there and give it your all and see what happens. I gave all I had and unfortunately it just wasn't enough. That's just part of playing the game."

In the next match, Justin Leonard was 4-up after four holes — but didn't win. Denmark's Thomas Bjorn rallied for a halve.

Of the next eight matches, the United States won six, lost one, and halved one. The Ryder Cup had come down to this: The United States needed 1½ points from Woods, Love, and Leonard — three golfers who won major championships in 1997 — and got only a half, from Leonard. Together, they posted an overall 1-9-3 record, with the only victory coming from Woods in the opening bestball match with Mark O'Meara. The final score was Europe 14½ points, United States of America 13½ points.

The Americans were dumbfounded. "I knew Tiger's match and my match would be important," said Love, whose Ryder Cup record before Valderrama was 5-4 and 2-0 in singles. "He hung in there and I tried to. We played a lot better than it looked. It's a disappointing week for a lot of us, but especially me."

Lehman stood along the near wall of the media center and spoke at length about the results and his teammates. "I'm still totally convinced we have the 12 best players," he said. "Today proved that. But put their guys together and they have magic at their fingertips. The sum is greater than the parts. I'm proud that we fought back so hard. Very, very proud. If we could have pulled it off, it would have been one of the biggest comebacks in the history of any sport."

The point that clinched at least a tie came from Bernhard Langer's victory over Brad Faxon. It wasn't until the final match on the course, when Colin Montgomerie halved his match with Scott Hoch, that Europe got the additional half-point necessary to claim outright victory. Montgomerie's 3-1-1 record for 3½ points earned him Man of the Match honors.

"My caddie and I became aware at around the 12th or 13th hole that it might come down to us," Montgomerie said. "I was quite happy when I was No. 10 [in the singles order], thinking it would be just a walk in the park, but it didn't turn out that way. We all had to keep going."

Seve Ballesteros got the customary congratulatory phone call from King Juan Carlos. "He told me he's very happy," Ballesteros said. "He's been following it on TV and he said he got very nervous when things looked complicated."

Ballesteros then held a mini news conference, announcing that he would not return as captain in 1999. "For the simple reason that I want to get my own game back," he said.

Woods was the only American to play in the maximum five matches. He never had his "A" game — more like C+ — and his 1-3-1 record was indicative of how he played. For historical perspective, Jack Nicklaus was 1-2-1 in his Ryder Cup debut, and Arnold Palmer was 3-0-1 as a rookie. Palmer, who has the highest Ryder Cup winning percentage among Americans, was 6-3-2 in his 11 singles matches. "You wouldn't guess it," Tom Lehman said. "Jack Nicklaus got beat. Arnie got beat. Tom Watson got beat. Just because you're the best player doesn't mean you can't lose."

"I guess what I take away from this — it's just like everyone else — a chance for all of us to get really close to one another. It was a bonding experience. I can't believe the way these guys are — they're awesome. I'm just thankful to have these guys around. I'm just thankful to have these eleven guys and an awesome captain."

October

Hide 'n' Go Seek

Walt Disney World/Oldsmobile Classic
Disney World
Lake Buena Vista, Florida
October 16–19

"Just another golfer." That's how Greg Norman described Tiger Woods. The comments came in a prerecorded interview to promote an Australian tournament, The Players Championship, at Norman's home course of Royal Queensland in December. Give Norman credit. He knows how to get attention and the "just another golfer" line got plenty. Predictably so.

Norman's evaluation of Woods' 1997 performance followed the Ryder Cup Matches. With most of the PGA Tour on guard against making controversial comments about Woods, it certainly was out of the ordinary.

"Tiger got off to a phenomenal fast start, but he's come back to reality and he's just another golfer out there, like all of us, who's going to have his ups and downs," Norman said. "In any profession when there's a lot of hype, the individuals that play the game understand that, and in a career like golf it takes decades to really smooth itself out and see how good you are over a period of time. The hype has put him up on a level, and now, the way his play is, it's not up to that level and the hype has calmed down."

Norman had made similar remarks back in August about the hype, saying a player was whatever the media made him out to be, or not to be. William Shakespeare never said it more eloquently. But had the hype really calmed down?

Tiger Woods' return to the PGA Tour after the Ryder Cup marked his initial appearance as a defending champion. A scheduling change set up Woods' first defense at the site of his second victory. He broke into the winner's circle at the Las Vegas Invitational two weeks before the 1996 Walt Disney World/Oldsmobile Classic.

But before Woods put a peg in the ground in defense of his title, another international star made headlines. This time, it was Scotland's Colin Montgomerie, who had fired broadsides at the Americans in Spain and in the wake of the Ryder Cup had been ripped in the United States for insensitive remarks. Americans didn't appreciate his comments about Brad Faxon, Scott Hoch, and Tiger Woods, and said so. A couple even suggested that Montgomerie would be wise to reconsider his desire to play in America because he had no friends on the U.S. PGA Tour.

Montgomerie, while representing Scotland at the Dunhill Cup at the Old Course in St. Andrews, sent letters of apology to some members of the U.S. Ryder Cup team and issued a public statement explaining his comments. Montgomerie called the initiative an attempt to present a "more balanced view of the issues." He said his remarks, in response to an inquiry from a journalist, "did not come out as I intended and I regret that this has occurred." He continued, "I especially regret the personal nature of remarks about members of the [U.S.] team. I have written to each person on the American Team who was named in the press and to Captain Tom Kite, and I have made special efforts to discuss this situation with Brad Faxon and I shall always be grateful to him and shall respect his understanding which, under such circumstances, has been so professional."

The most intense criticism of Montgomerie had come for saying Faxon "is going through a divorce, and mentally I don't think he will be with it." Montgomerie said his words, at the very least, had been taken out of context and distorted. He restated his "great respect" for the U.S. Ryder Cup Team.

Woods had other things on his mind. He was trying to shake a slump that had stretched nearly four months, since his victory at the Western Open in July. But just as the Ryder Cup served to humanize the phenom, so had the second half of the PGA Tour season. He wasn't winning, but he was learning and in some quarters he was becoming infinitely more likable. He was no longer impervious to human frailty, and that made him more like the rest of us.

The victory curve was downward, but a more important curve was headed up. A transformation that began months before was continuing. He wasn't making all the putts he made in January, April, May or July. He was trying to force things on the golf course and, as a result, often didn't play with the poise or patience that had marked that historic victory at Augusta National. He was a 21-year-old golfer acting — for a change — like a 21-year-old golfer.

The assessment of Woods' ability and potential didn't change during the slump. It was enhanced. The bar was set not lower, but even higher. The kid was learning and maturing. It was obvious in his demeanor, in his posture, in his words. He was going to win again, and win big. It was just a matter of time.

"Some of these people expect you to win every time, and so do I. But when you go out, give it your all and you don't win, that's sports.

"Overall, this has been, obviously, a great year. I haven't been playing as good as I would like of late. And I think the last few months that's probably just due to the fact that I'm not used to playing this much golf.

"I think I didn't pace myself correctly early in the year. This was all new to me so I'm going to make some mistakes and obviously I did. I didn't spread out my schedule enough."

Woods won the Disney in 1996 with a final round 66 for a 267 total, 21 under par. He outlasted veteran Payne Stewart. Another youngster, Taylor Smith, matched Woods but was disqualified for using a putter with a nonconforming grip. The Disney is played on three courses — Lake Buena Vista, Magnolia, and Palm. They're relatively easy tracks, the kind Woods devours when he's on his game. The Disney and the Las Vegas Invitational the following week were the perfect places for Woods to relocate his game. In golf's elusive game of hide 'n' go seek, he was getting warm.

"My game is coming back. We found some positions that were off, corrected them, and am getting back to the position where I was

at the beginning of this year, when I was hitting the ball the best I've hit it."

Woods didn't find it at the Disney. Stewart, who lives in Orlando and plays his best golf there, led with a first-round 64, 8 under par over the Palm Course. He won the tournament in 1983 and always seems to finish in the top five. Woods got off to a nice start. He made birdie on the final two holes on the Palm for 66. It's no secret what it takes to win the Disney — birdies, birdies, and more birdies. It's a shoot-out, and the hottest putter prevails.

"If you don't putt well, you're not going to win — period. This tournament is about who makes the most birdies."

Woods was positioned perfectly. His second round in the rotation of three courses was scheduled for Lake Buena Vista, where he shot 63 the year before. It could have been even lower, and Woods had that on his mind when he teed it up. He had a chance to make a move — and it wasn't even Saturday.

Stewart was on the same rotation and toured Lake Buena Vista in 67 strokes, 5 under, but felt awkward doing it. He had left too many strokes out there. However, he still had a 2-shot lead. Woods fell off the pace. He made bogey twice early in the round, shot 71, and fell 6 shots behind Stewart. Woods' distance control was off — he missed the first three greens long.

"I got gun-shy."

The 71 was eight shots more than he had taken at LBV in 1996. "If you don't pay attention at Lake Buena Vista, it can jump up and get you," Stewart said. "I think Mr. Woods would probably attest to that. He'd probably like to have my score, and I'd like to be a little better."

Woods played better in Round III, but the tournament was slipping away. He shot 70 when the leaders were in the 60s and slipped to 9 shots behind the new leader, Len Mattiace. Stewart remained in contention, and also lurking was David Duval, who shed the bridesmaid image a week earlier at Kingsmill by finally breaking into the winner's circle with a playoff victory. Duval, a Floridian, would have tied for the lead after three rounds except for a final-hole bogey on the Palm course.

Duval, 25, is another in the first tier of young players on the PGA Tour. At Georgia Tech, he became one of only three four-time Division I First-Team All-Americans (Phil Mickelson and Gary Hallberg were the others). He won $881,436 as a Tour rookie in 1995, finishing second three times, and another $977,079 in 1996. All that was missing was a victory. The omission was corrected at the Michelob Championships at Kingsmill in Williamsburg, Virginia, and he backed it up in Orlando with another playoff victory. It made him the third golfer to win back-to-back events in 1997. The others were Mark O'Meara at AT&T Pebble Beach and the Buick Invitational, and Ernie Els at the U.S. Open and the Buick Classic.

Duval defeated Dan Forsman in sudden death with a 15-foot putt for par on the first extra hole. Duval shot a final round 70 for 270. The $270,000 prize pushed him past the $1 million mark. What Duval already knew was confirmed in his two victories — sometimes there is often only a sliver of difference between winning and losing, and the intangible in the formula is often good fortune. Duval had the feel and look of a winner in the final round, and he got the breaks.

Woods had a bit role in the last act. He shot 71, for a 10-under-par 278, and finished tied for 26th. Greg Norman wasn't around to evaluate the performance.

The Right Stuff

Las Vegas Invitational
TPC of Summerlin
Las Vegas, Nevada
October 22–26

Tiger Woods' title defense at the Las Vegas Invitational began with a joyride at 570 miles per hour. It was his Chuck Yeager impersonation. Woods spent a half hour soaring across the skies in an F-16 fighter jet piloted by Major Randy Lane of the Air Force Thunderbirds. The flight was smoother than Woods' golf. It was so smooth the major offered Woods the controls on the way home — with just a little help.

On the golf front, the PGA of America announced that Woods had clinched its Player of the Year Award, which is based on a point system. The PGA Tour Player of the Year Award, announced in January, is voted on by members of the Tour. Woods' four victories helped him to 98 points, 28 more than Davis Love III, in the PGA of America version of the honor.

The '96 victory in Las Vegas catapulted Woods to a phenomenal first 12 months on the PGA Tour. He did it with terrific golf and plenty of savvy. He rallied with a final round 64, 8 under par, to match Love's total, and then won on the first sudden death hole. The world of professional golf hasn't been the same since, and likely won't be for many years to come.

Woods' triumph in Las Vegas assured him a place on the PGA Tour and eliminated the need to try the Qualifying School. In late-season tournaments, the Q-School is foremost on the minds of golfers battling to finish in the top 125. It was no different at Las Vegas, with the golfers jockeying for position. With the schedule change, which put Las Vegas immediately before The Tour Championship, it also meant Vegas was the last chance for those attempting to qualify for the final official event of the season. The Tour Championship matches the top 30 golfers on the money list for the biggest purse on Tour, a cool $4 million. Those two races got as much attention as the tournament.

"Certain guys are trying to save their lives and certain guys are trying to get into the Tour Championship," said Billy Andrade, who was 30th on the money list. "I'm the bubble man and I want to play next week."

When Woods returned to Las Vegas for the 1997 tournament, there was something decidedly different. This time, he was old enough to gamble and drink. But breaking the bank wasn't his focus. He was preoccupied with golf and, later in the week, with his health.

Woods, playing at Desert Inn Country Club, opened with a strong 68. It was 3 shots better than his '96 start and it had Woods thinking good thoughts about the weekend.

"It wasn't too bad. I hit a lot of good shots today. I'm feeling great."

It was Phil Mickelson was who feeling in the pink in Round II. Lefty reeled off seven straight birdies to shoot 28 on the front in a 63, 9 under par, at TPC of Summerlin. The weather was perfect and 63 was a popular number — there were three, and five 64s — as the scoring heated up. "Obviously, I was thinking 59," Mickelson said. The scoring was so low that Woods shot 64 at Las Vegas Country Club, for a two-round total of 12 under, but was four shots off the pace. Woods had an eagle at the par 5 9th hole and back-to-back birdies to finish the round.

"It feels good to get back in the tournament. I'm enjoying this. I'm glad to get my game going in a more positive flow."

Everything changed in the third round. The wind started blowing and the weather cooled dramatically, but Woods' temperature soared. He was suffering from a 103-degree fever during the third round, which explained his erratic play. Woods made two double-bogeys on the front, wasted shots around the greens, and shot 77, not a bad number at the craps table but snake eyes on a golf course. Woods wasn't alone. Mickelson suffered a 16-shot swing, from 63 to 79. The winds gusted to 45 miles per hour — not quite F-16 force but enough to send scores, and temperatures, ballistic. Duffy Waldorf didn't know what was going on. He was playing at Desert Inn, where there are no leaderboards. He kept plugging along, ignorant to the crashes around him. Waldorf shot 69 to gain a 4-shot lead.

The weather again was dismal in the fourth round, but Waldorf clung to the lead, although it was cut in half. Not a single golfer shot in the 60s Saturday, when the stroke average was 74.457. Woods beat it, with 71, but he fell out of contention and the next day wound up tied for 36th. In 20 events, only once did he finish worse — that a tie for 43rd at the Buick Classic in June. Woods shot a final round 75 to finish at 355, 5 under par, in the unsuccessful title defense in Las Vegas. That was 15 strokes short of the winner, Bill Glasson, a man who knows all about adversity. Glasson, back on Tour after a recent surgery, registered a 66 at the TPC of Summerlin.

The victory, and $324,000 first prize, put Glasson into the top 30 — and into the elite Tour Championship field. Andrade finished 31st, less than $5 behind Andrew Magee at No. 30. "I woke up and I had a good feeling," Glasson said. "It was a struggle during the middle rounds. After surviving those two days, I saw the weather was calm. I knew I — or anyone — could go low."

Except, of course, Tiger Woods, the man who had gone sky high to start the week.

Trick or Treat

The Tour Championship
Champions Golf Club
Houston, Texas
October 30–November 2

*T*he Tour Championship is the final event of the season. The purse is $4 million, with $720,000 to the winner. Appropriately, since eligibility is based on the money list, it's the most lucrative payday on the PGA Tour. The field is limited to the top 30 and last place is worth $64,000. When the elite group arrived at Champions Golf Club, 13 golfers already had won at least $1 million in 1997. At the top of the list was Tiger Woods, at $1,969,233, and he was assured of becoming the first PGA Tour player to surpass $2 million in a single season. It's reflective of the kind of season Woods produced that in some respects it ended on a disappointing note. After all, before the summer swoon he was a candidate to go directly to $3 million.

Only two others in the field at Champions had a chance to pass Woods to win the money crown — No. 2 Justin Leonard ($1,463,531) and No. 3 Davis Love III ($1,359,953). Everyone in the top 30 who wasn't already there also had a chance to reach the $1 million mark at The Tour Championship.

The backdrop for all this was a plummeting stock market. There was an economic crisis in Asia and in the last week of October, Wall Street was reeling from the aftershocks. Wall Street doesn't call the phenomenon a slump. It's called a correction. Nobody was calling Woods' summer slippage a correction when, upon further review, that's exactly what it was.

Clearly, there was no decline on the worldwide professional golf exchange. The bull market continued and more prosperity was on the way.

Two days before the start of The Tour Championship, Commissioner Tim Finchem announced in Houston the new World Golf Championships series to commence in 1999. The PGA Tours International Federation, a collaboration of the PGA, European, Southern Africa, Australasian, and Japan tours, developed what amounts to a world tour. Each event would have a purse of at least $4 million, like The Tour Championship, and all would be limited field competitions. Even bigger paydays were on the horizon for golf's international stars. With all the prize money from the World Golf Championships considered "official" earnings and the previously announced purse increases on the PGA Tour, existing earnings records would soon be relics. It would be nothing for someone like Ernie Els or Greg Norman or Colin Montgomerie or Tiger Woods — especially Tiger Woods — to win $4 million a year.

But Woods was not thinking about 1999, or even 1998. Not yet. There was still some unfinished business in 1997. Besides, there was an historic year to savor. There was no rush to see it end. The Tour Championship is a celebration for the best of the best — golf's Top Guns — and Woods warmed to the occasion.

"It's a big tournament, obviously. It's the only time when we play for a purse this big, and also you get the best players on our Tour. We have all the top 30 here, and as of right now, I think about at least 20 of them are playing really good golf. So with that in mind, it's going to be a great shoot-out."

Woods' appearance at The Tour Championship in 1996 at Southern Hills Country Club in Tulsa was part of the fairy tale that was his first two months on the PGA Tour. However, the experience was ruined by the illness of his father.

"Last year was one of those weeks you want to forget because of what happened to my dad. This week is different. He's here. He's in town, and this time he's in good health. And my game is coming around nicely, and I'm really looking forward to playing."

Woods' pre-tournament press conference was a review of his season, with emphasis on his growth as a golfer and his relationship to others on the PGA Tour. In Spain, he talked about the Ryder Cup being a bonding experience with other members of the United States team. He picked up on the theme in Houston.

"You come back and you can call each other up, say how are you guys doing? I know I have more lunches with these guys now because of that...we play more practice rounds together. You can talk on a (different) level now that you know these guys. You can talk more freely, more openly, and more cordially."

Justin Leonard teamed with Tiger in an alternate shot partnership at the Ryder Cup. "I got to know him quite a bit better and I think a lot of the guys did," Leonard said. "I would have said we were friends before that but not knowing him all that well. I think I've got a much better sense of where he comes from now and look forward to getting together and playing and then doing things off the course." After the Ryder Cup, Fred Couples had echoed similar sentiments. "A lot of us wanted to see what Tiger was all about," said Couples, who didn't make the field for The Tour Championship. "We didn't really know him and now we know he's a great guy." Woods also claimed to be more comfortable around the media.

"Totally. I was — how can I put it? — a little more distant probably after The Masters. I was just getting bombarded so much that everything I was kind of saying was being used and sometimes twisted, and that became very tough for me to handle.

"Then I said, You know what? This (the media scrutiny) is a fact. It's reality. Just go out there and be yourself and just say the things that come to your mind that are just you and that are real. And whatever they do with it, that's whatever they do with it. And because of that attitude change, things have just come to flow out of me. Now you see me more comfortable in the press room. You see me more comfortable playing with amateurs on Pro-Am days. I've just become used to the whole thing, and it's been great. I think this is a maturing process, and it happens to a lot of people who are my age."

The new outlook notwithstanding, Woods was anticipating the end of the official season, which was just five days away.

"I'm putting the sticks up for a while and it's going to be nice. It will be a great break."

$\mathscr{O} \mathscr{O}$

*T*he hottest player in the game, David Duval, shared the first-round lead with Jim Furyk and Sweden's Jesper Parnevik, who arrived at Champions Golf Club with an assortment of swings. Parnevik selected the right one and his 66, 5-under-par, matched Duval and Furyk. Brad Faxon was a shot back with five others at 68. Tiger Woods shot 69, 2-under.

If the back-to-back victories in October meant Duval had unearthed the secret, he wasn't telling. Meanwhile, there was no secret for Parnevik. He stumbled onto something — again — that worked and he was riding it. How often does he change? "Oh, every day," Parnevik said. "Might be a new swing tomorrow. That's the toughest thing about this game. It's not only you who lose it overnight. We lose it as well. You're happy if you fire balls on the range and it's still there from the previous day. Otherwise, you're in for a tough day again. I'm so used to changing every day."

Furyk's swing may not be much to look at but it repeats, and had for most of the 1997 season. Furyk and Faxon were among those surprised to see such low scores. But Champions, which has been host to the U.S. Open and the Ryder Cup, was playing shorter than its 7,220 yards, and it was vulnerable.

Woods knew he was getting close to peak form again and a solid first round was his confirmation. He went from the 18th green to the scorer's trailer to the practice tee where, under the watchful eye of Butch Harmon, he hit balls until dusk. In one sequence, he hit eight balls so tightly grouped that from an angle behind and to the right, it looked like they were all a single ball. Woods nodded, hit another shot, listened to Harmon and smiled. The phenom was in his element now, hitting balls in near darkness, and Shivas Irons, the central character of author Michael Murphy's classic tale, "Golf in the Kingdom," came to mind. Woods' swing was smooth and easy. The balls leaped off the clubface and, in the dimming light, landed softly off in the distance.

The crowd had thinned out. The bleachers behind the driving range were virtually empty but when Woods turned to leave, there was a sudden surge of bodies scrambling toward him from out of nowhere. There were dozens of kids, all calling out his name and pleading for an autograph. Woods signed his name a few times and answered a couple of questions. He left Champions Golf Club feeling good about the state of his game.

☙ ❧

A golfer in a red shirt lit up Champions in Round II. But it wasn't Sunday and it wasn't Tiger. It was Scott Hoch, the underrated Scott Hoch.

"Without a doubt. This guy has some serious game. He's not in the limelight...he's one of the best iron players out here."

Hoch made bogey at the 18th hole to shoot 65 for 133, 9-under, and a 1-shot lead over Jim Furyk and two better than David Duval and Mark Calcavecchia. Dave Love III and Brad Faxon were at 136, followed by Woods and Glasson, who were 4 shots behind Hoch.

Fact is, if Woods' putter had gotten hot, he might have shot 64 himself instead of 68. On the back nine, he had birdie chance after birdie chance and never made any.

Woods registered an eagle at the 9th hole, a 509-yard par 5 where he chipped in to get to 5-under.

"It was a little bump-and-run 9-iron. I hit it too hard but the fringe stopped it pretty good, which I was thankful for. From there it was dead downgrain, downhill. It started picking up speed, and I wondered if I hit it too hard where the speed wasn't going to take the break. It took the break and went right in the middle."

Woods is a momentum golfer and it looked like that would set him up for a back-nine flurry. His putter let him down.

"It's just a matter of time if I can keep hitting the ball as well as I'm hitting it right now. I played well the entire back nine. I hit the ball the best I've hit it since I've been here. But I didn't make a thing. I couldn't throw a pea in the ocean. I hit some good putts on the back nine but then I misread them. When I had the good reads, I hit them horrible. It was just a frustrating back nine.

"I couldn't make a damn thing. It was horrible. Absolutely horrible."

But it wasn't hard to find a silver lining. His game was back, and he had the weekend to confirm it.

"Hoch is going really low. You want to keep pace. You don't want to get too far behind with two rounds to go. You want to be up there in position to make a run. If I would have putted halfway decent, I would have been up there in the lead.

"My iron play finally came around. It was nice to hit some nice, crisp irons, hit the ball the right distance with a nice trajectory. I just couldn't take advantage of it.

"We've got 36 holes. That's a long, long way to go. If Hoch can hit 10-under in 36 holes, so can we. You never know."

With that, Woods hurried to the practice putting green, where he was joined by Harmon and Fluff Cowan. Harmon worked on body position, especially the alignment of Woods' shoulders. It paid off sooner than Woods expected. Woods, sans costume on Halloween Night, attended the Houston Rockets' 1997–98 NBA season opener against Cleveland, compliments of good friend Charles Barkley. The trick was on Tiger, the treat for the basketball fans. Woods was introduced to the crowd and called down to hit a putt during a break in the action. He drained it.

"That was a complete set-up. I had no clue 'til they put it in front of me. That was a big putt."

ॐ ॐ

There was no resemblance between the way Tiger Woods finished the second round and the way he started the third at Champions Golf Club. The wind picked up and turned around. "Such a big difference from the way it played the first two days," said Jesper Parnevik, who shot 69 for 208. Champions is Steve Elkington's home course. Elk was 3-under through 36 holes. He didn't mind the wind. "I needed it to blow a little bit to catch some people off-guard," he said. "I know the course so well, it doesn't bother me."

It was troublesome, indeed, and there was plenty of volatility on the leaderboard. With all that money at stake, it looked a little like the stock market...but not necessarily a bull market. "It was a bear out there," said Brad Faxon, one of the four leaders at 8-under-par. Faxon (69) was joined at 205 by Bill Glasson (68), Davis Love III (69), and David Duval (70). Scott Hoch shot 74 and Woods had 75.

The un-Tiger like behavior was a concern to his fans who were also watching Woods' playing partner, Glasson, make birdies. "How come Tiger can't make one of those (good) shots?" a young fan asked. Woods' only birdie came on the par 5 5th hole. He couldn't even make birdie at the 9th, a hole he eagled the day before. On moving day, it was not a good omen.

"It was blowing pretty hard out there. We had some problems with the trees swirling. The wind was getting into the trees and really doing a number on the ball. You had to keep a lot of short irons low and that's kind of hard sometimes. I had a couple of up-shooters that never came close to getting to the green. That's what happens when you play in this wind. You've got to hit the ball very solid, very crisp."

Woods made double-bogey 6 at the first hole and a three-putt bogey at the third. The real crusher came at the 12th, a difficult 209-yard par 3 over an expanse of water, where his 3-iron shot ballooned into the breeze and plopped into the hazard.

"I was right there. I was back in the ballgame. What really hurt me was not the double on No. 1, but the double on 12. I got the momentum by birdieing the 10th, then I thought if I made par there, I could go ahead and make birdie at 13 and get back in the game. I wasn't able to do that...consequently, here I am over-par for the day."

The wind was blowing so hard — with gusts up to 25 to 30 miles per hour — it made putting an adventure. Duval altered his game plan on the greens as a result. "I changed my approach a little bit in that I wasn't as aggressive on my first putts because with that wind you don't want to stand over three- and four-footers all day coming back to make pars." In stronger winds, staying in balance over a putt becomes a challenge.

There was nothing unsteady about Woods after the disappointing round. Where a few months ago he probably would have pouted and whisked past the media waiting for a post-round utterance, that wasn't the case anymore. Woods stood there and answered the questions with almost as much spit and polish as a Michael Jordan. The talk about a rising comfort level with the media wasn't just lip service. Woods was backing it up.

With Justin Leonard failing to mount a challenge, only Love had a chance to pass Woods on the money list and the results of Saturday's round thrust that possibility into the spotlight. The first-place check of $720,000 would put Love at $2,079,953, meaning that Woods would need a finish of 10th or better, with 10th place worth $113,600, to stay ahead. After 54 holes, Woods was 19th in the field of 30 golfers. While all athletes insist the trophy is more important than the money, $720,000 is quite a carrot.

"Protecting your position on the money list is on a lot of guys' minds," said Love, who was No. 3. "You have to fight that urge to think about what can happen; think about the golf. There's a bunch of guys with a chance to win. The guy who is thinking most about golf, concentrating on what he's doing, is going to win. The guy who is thinking about money is not going to be able to keep up. It's hard not to think about a purse like this. It's part of the challenge of winning."

There was more to this debate. A victory by Love at The Tour Championship could have ramifications when the PGA Tour players sat down to mark their ballots for Player of the Year. Woods had been the odds-on favorite since January but Love's late-season surge, if it included The Tour Championship, could narrow the gap significantly. Did Love still have a shot? "Got me," he said. "Worry about that tomorrow...I don't know. He played well in the majors. Winning The Masters by that many, I mean, it's hard not to vote for him, no matter what happens this week."

If that sounded like a concession speech, it wasn't the first of the week. Woods delivered one of his own when he said he couldn't catch Nick Price in the race for the Vardon Trophy, which is awarded annually by the PGA of America to the golfer with the lowest adjusted scoring average over a minimum of 60 rounds. The list of winners reflects the greatness and importance of the award — Jimmy Demaret, Ben Hogan, Sam Snead, Arnold Palmer, Lee Trevino, Tom Kite, Raymond Floyd, Greg Norman, and Fred Couples among them. Nick Price, who won the Vardon in 1993, held a slight edge over Woods. Price's cushion was about a dozen shots and the third-round swing in Price's favor (he shot 73) meant there was no chance at all for Woods.

The 1997 PGA Tour season was going down to its final round. The 18 holes at Champions Golf Club on Sunday, November 2, were going to have an enormous impact on the post-season honors.

ॐ ॐ

Despite shooting 75 to finish tied for 26th with Lee Janzen and Ernie Els at 289, Nick Price captured his second Vardon Trophy. "You don't 'fluke' the Vardon Trophy," Price said. "You've got to go out there and play solid all year.... It is really humbling to have your name associated with those who have won this award." The final adjusted stroke averages: Price 68.98, Woods 69.10, and Greg Norman 69.16.

There's nothing 'fluke' about three straight victories, either. At The Tour Championship, David Duval became the first player since Price in 1993 to win three consecutive starts and, in so doing, put himself on Tiger Woods' Christmas gift list. At the top of it, actually, because that's where Duval put Woods — on top.

The final round was rife with speculation and permutations. Everything was going on. Davis Love III broke out of a four-way tie with birdies on the first two holes and opened up a 2-shot lead. Duval and Jim Furyk didn't give up the ghost, but when Love made the turn at 11-under and Woods was finishing with a bogey at No. 18 to shoot 69-281, the permutations added up to this:

Love was in position to win the tournament and, in a most dramatic fashion, usurp the title of the PGA Tour's money leader for 1997 from Woods. When Woods walked off the final green, it was clear he wouldn't finish in the requisite two-way tie for 10th, or better, and win the needed $110,000 to clinch the honor. He ended in a tie for 12th with Greg Norman and Scott McCarron to win $97,600. Woods' only hope was for somebody to catch Love, and the candidates to do that were dwindling. Only Duval and Furyk were left. Woods wasn't going to win the money title, or so he thought. So did most others.

"I'm kind of pissed off about that right now. I knew about it on the 14th green. I knew I had to get to 5-under and just wasn't able to do it. To have this good a year and not be on top really does hurt because I played so well for most of the year, winning a major, winning four times this year, going over $2 million. To end up like this, it does hurt."

A Love victory also would have put a new spin on PGA Tour Player of the Year projections. Woods certainly would remain the front-runner but Love's name would be in the mix and it wouldn't be difficult to make a case for either when the players marked their ballots. On his side of the ledger, Love had a stronger finish, a major triumph at the PGA Championship, what would have been a third triumph with The Tour Championship and a huge payday, plus some important intangibles. He's among the most popular golfers — maybe the single most popular — on Tour and a player director on the PGA Tour Policy Board. Woods was asked what he thought.

"I don't know. You've got to ask the other players. Now is not a good time to ask that."

Woods had to pack for a flight, and return home before a trip to Japan the following week. He should have stuck around. It was quite a finish.

Duval, 25, eagled the par 5 13th hole to climb into the lead at 11-under-par with Love. Furyk made four birdies in a seven-hole stretch and reached 10-under at the 15th, leaving those three golfers separated by 1 shot. Love's bogey at the 14th dropped him back to 10-under and left Duval to lead alone. Duval made an heroic par save at the 17th, after driving into the right rough where his ball was only about six feet from being out of bounds. He made another par save after driving into the left rough at the 18th. Duval's 68, for 273, gave him a 1-shot victory over Furyk with Love, who made bogey at the final hole, another shot back.

Duval won $720,000, Furyk $432,000, and Love $276,000 — and gave Woods the money title with $2,066,833. Duval jumped into second at $1,885,308, followed by Love at $1,635,953, Furyk $1,619,480, and Justin Leonard $1,587,531.

In the interview room, Love gave the media the sound bite it was looking for.

"I would have liked to have finished a little better, obviously," he said. "But it was nice to have a chance. Nice to at least make Tiger a little nervous there with nine holes to go." With three-year-old son Davis IV on his lap, Love expressed his disappointment at missing the shot at Player of the Year. "If I had a chance, that's disappointing," he said. "I had a good year. Tiger, come U.S. Open time, nobody really had a chance at Player of the Year other than him. So it was nice to at least get myself in the running. He played so well all year long that he deserved it. And the money title...I've been close before. Second's better than third. First has a different ring to it."

Duval's opinion on the subject: "If the outcome had been different this week and Davis won, my vote still would have been for Tiger because Tiger seemed to play better through the course of the whole year. I think you've got to remember it is Player of the Year. But it probably would have become a lot closer. I might have thought about it a little more."

David Duval probably would have gotten some votes, too. From Eldrick Woods, for sure.

Duval's streak started in Virginia at the Michelob Championship at Kingsmill and he backed it up at the Walt Disney World/Oldsmobile

Classic. He skipped the Las Vegas Invitational the following week and returned for the season finale. With the victory at Champions he became the first player in PGA Tour history to collect his first three wins in consecutive starts. It was another breakthrough for golf's young lions, another in the series of successes authored by Tiger Woods, Justin Leonard, Ernie Els, and the PGA Tour's other twenty-something superstars.

Tiger Woods played in 21 official events in 1997, winning an average of nearly $100,000 an event. He won four times, including an historic victory at The Masters, plus the money title and the PGA of America's Player of the Year honor. He was destined to add the PGA Tour's Player of the Year award, and likely others.

Golf archivists will bookmark 1997 as the Year of the Tiger, and the emergence of cosmic golf — but Tiger Woods can't be defined by a moment in time. Great adventures are never subject to boundaries. The journey continues.